The Official Scrabble® Players® Handbook

Edited by
Drue K. Conklin
Scrabble® Crossword Game Players®, Inc.

Harmony Books
A Division of Crown Publishers, Inc.
New York

Library of Congress Catalogue Card Number: 75-41719
ISBN: 0-517-525461 cloth
ISBN: 0-517-52547X pbk.

Publisher:
Harmony Books
A Division of Crown Publishers, Inc.
419 Park Avenue South
New York, NY 10016
Published simultaneously in Canada
by General Publishing Company Limited.

Printed in the United States of America.

Acknowledgment

This Handbook was made possible through the hard work of many different people. In particular, we would like to thank Mr. Michael J. Senkiewicz whose expertise went into the tactics and strategy, and Miss Drue K. Conklin who pulled the Handbook together.

Scrabble® Crossword Game Players,® Inc.

Table Of Contents

Introduction

This Handbook is designed to give SCRABBLE Crossword Game lovers a thorough introduction to new avenues of the game. Avenues that have never been explored or exposed.

Part 1 concentrates on what SCRABBLE Crossword Game Players is and what it can offer you. SCRABBLE PLAYERS was not designed to cater only to expert players but to reach out to all levels of game lovers. Whether you're fiercely competitive or prefer a social game, SCRABBLE PLAYERS has something of interest to offer you.

By tightening up the rules for club and tournament play, SCRABBLE PLAYERS is not suggesting that everyone must use these rules. Many players prefer to stick with the box rules or their own variations. People should play at home by the rules of their choosing. But just a word of caution . . . all players should agree on the ground rules *before* the game begins.

Part 2 of this work tells how best to profit from the Handbook according to your own level of expertise. Of interest to many players is the section entitled "Questions & Answers: Playing Procedures." Be sure to pay special attention to Chapter 5—The SCRABBLE PLAYERS Notational System.

As in many games, SCRABBLE Crossword Game contains an element of luck. But the luck element is not enough to override a player's superior skill to make winning or losing a random result. However, it is enough to allow a poorer player to score an occasional victory over a better player by virtue of being lucky.

This combination of luck and skill makes SCRABBLE Crossword Game the popular pastime that it is, since every competitor has some hope of success. But don't forget . . . good players can also be lucky and the element of chance always evens out in the long run.

Much more important than the luck of the draw is what a player does with the tiles he has drawn. As in all games, the SCRABBLE Crossword Game player is beset with two ever-present problems:

1) What to do?
2) How to do it?

The first problem may be defined as strategy; the second, as tactics.

Strategy is planning the conduct of the game. Tactics pertain to the devices used to implement the strategy. Strategy is abstract; tactics, concrete. Because of this, many SCRABBLE Crossword Game players are inclined to put little or no emphasis on strategy and concentrate totally upon tactics. Yet both problems are always present, and, in fact, inseparable.

Both strategy and tactics are thoroughly discussed in the Handbook. Then, to bring all aspects of this work together, six completely annotated games are presented. Each play is carefully analyzed to show what is bad, good, or would have been better.

So that every player may test the newly acquired principles of the Handbook, each person is invited to try the quizzes found in Part 7. Just in case you happen to miss one or two, each problem has an answer and a suggested chapter for review.

All in all, the SCRABBLE PLAYERS Handbook is a complete discussion of the game from the opening move right down to the last tile. The best plan of attack is to read the book from cover to cover and then return to sections which are of special interest to you.

Good luck! Here's to many exciting games ahead.

Scrabble® Crossword Game Players,® Inc.

Part 1

SCRABBLE Crossword Game Players, Inc. is a communications network which spreads the "word" to SCRABBLE Crossword Game lovers. This first part of the Handbook deals with questions that many people have asked:

- What does membership in SCRABBLE PLAYERS offer?
- How does someone start a licensed club?
- What is a trademark?
- Who invented SCRABBLE Crossword Game?

These and many more questions are answered in this section.

DEPARTMENT OF RECREATION PARKS ADMINISTRATION
SCRABBLE® PLAYERS CENTER

What Is Scrabble® Crossword Game Players,® Inc.?

Chapter 1

SCRABBLE Crossword Game players are men, women, and children of every age, height, weight, interest, and IQ—a variety of people playing at every level, sharing a boundless enthusiasm for the game. So much enthusiasm, that we were inspired to form a national organization called SCRABBLE PLAYERS. It now has thousands of members from all over the USA and Canada—all sharing a keen interest in the game. And we'd like to welcome you.

Officially, we're SCRABBLE Crossword Game Players, Inc., a wholly-owned subsidiary of Selchow & Righter Company, the folks who own the trademark SCRABBLE. Our main purpose is to bring lovers of the game together. We do this through our publications as well as through sponsorship of official tournaments and licensed clubs.

With the start of public activities, we realized that the box rules would have to be tightened up so that everyone could be judged under the same conditions. The SCRABBLE PLAYERS Club and Tournament rules, found in Chapter 4, standardize playing procedures for people all around the country. This then enables us to answer questions that many of you have been asking: What is a good game score? A good turn score? These rules act as a yardstick so that, at last, players have a reliable, uniform way to compare their skills.

For those who would rather play more social games and who prefer to stick to the box rules, house rules, or game variations, SCRABBLE PLAYERS has a lot to offer you, too. Read on.

A. Membership

Membership dues in the national organization are $5.00 a year. For this you receive a SCRABBLE PLAYERS membership card and a full year's subscription to the SCRABBLE PLAYERS Newspaper.

The Newspaper is written for all types of players, whether you score 55 or 550! There are word lists with unusual words to spring on unsuspecting opponents; quizzes to tickle your brain; news about tournament activities; and articles featuring people like you. There are contests and puzzles and tips on strategy: when to bluff, how to challenge, what to do with poor tiles, how to use blanks, what to do with the Q . . . whether you are a home player or a tournament enthusiast, if you like the game, you will be interested in the SCRABBLE PLAYERS Newspaper.

Last, but not least, membership entitles you to receive black expert points for each game won at a SCRABBLE PLAYERS Club or Tournament. The more games you win, the more black points you accumulate. Eventually, when regional and national tournaments are underway, red and blue expert points will be awarded for special achievement.

How To Become A Member

To become a member of SCRABBLE Crossword Game Players, Inc. and receive: 1) your membership card, 2) a full year's subscription to the SCRABBLE PLAYERS Newspaper, and 3) expert points at a SCRABBLE PLAYERS Club or Tournament:

> Send a $5.00 check or money order to SCRABBLE PLAYERS, 200 Fifth Avenue, New York, NY 10010. If it's a gift, fill in the recipient's name and address, and include the giver's name.
>
> Please print: Name
Address
City
State or Province
Zip code

Canadian residents: Please send a postal money order in U.S. $5.00.

B. SCRABBLE PLAYERS Tournaments

SCRABBLE PLAYERS sponsors tournaments around the country through local recreation departments. Tournaments are run on a large scale—city-wide, county-wide, or state-wide and are free of charge to residents 16 years and older.

Tournaments are fun for all types of players. Scores range from 100 to 500 points. Members of SCRABBLE PLAYERS receive one expert point for each game won in both club and tournament play.

The first SCRABBLE PLAYERS Tournament was held in Brooklyn, New York in March of 1973. This tournament grew to become the New York City SCRABBLE PLAYERS Tournament where 2,000 residents turn out annually for this fall/spring competition. Other tournaments have been held in various cities around the country with new tournaments being set up every year. On the international front, 1975 ushered in the first Canadian SCRABBLE PLAYERS Tournament.

Do's and Don'ts for Tournaments

All SCRABBLE Crossword Game Tournaments:

- must be authorized by SCRABBLE PLAYERS
- are run through the recreation department
- are run according to SCRABBLE PLAYERS guidelines
- are run on a large scale—city-wide, county-wide, state-wide
- may not be used for fund raising or gambling

More information is available by writing to SCRABBLE PLAYERS, 200 Fifth Avenue, New York, NY 10010.

If you are interested in smaller scale activities, think about forming a licensed SCRABBLE PLAYERS Club. This is an enjoyable way for an organization or a smaller community to run weekly or semimonthly SCRABBLE PLAYERS sessions.

C. SCRABBLE PLAYERS Clubs

SCRABBLE PLAYERS is now licensing organizations, libraries, Y's, colleges, recreation departments, and individuals to set up and run SCRABBLE PLAYERS Clubs.

Just what is involved and what does it mean to you or to your organization?

First of all, SCRABBLE PLAYERS Clubs will be structured so that everyone throughout the country will be playing in the same way under the same rules and conditions. Whether players are beginners or experts, this will be a fun way of matching up people of equal ability to enjoy many good games.

1. Why Must Clubs Be Licensed?

SCRABBLE is a registered trademark of Selchow & Righter Company. It's a brand that identifies a variety of Selchow & Righter quality products and services.

Chess, checkers, and backgammon are in the public domain. They are generic. This means that anyone can manufacture these games; anyone can run a chess, checker, or backgammon club and tournament.

This is not the case with SCRABBLE Brand games. Only Selchow & Righter can manufacture them; only Selchow & Righter and its subsidiary, SCRABBLE PLAYERS, can run clubs and tournaments. Licensing people to use our trademark and run clubs ensures that the club will provide maximum enjoyment for its members.

2. How to Become a Licensed Club

It's not hard, but it does take a responsible person. Every SCRABBLE PLAYERS Club has an owner who signs a licensing agreement stating that he/she will protect the trademark, follow the Club Manual, not use the club for any charity fund raising purpose, gambling, etc.

Each SCRABBLE PLAYERS Club also has a certified director who runs every club session. The club director and club owner may be the same person—or different people. In either case, every club session *must* be run by a certified club director.

To become certified, the director must pass the director's test based on the SCRABBLE PLAYERS Club Manual. The test asks basic questions about club procedure, game rules, and other information from the Club Manual that is pertinent to running a good club. Since the director is the final arbiter in all club play, he/she must know the game and the rules very well. All club owners and directors must be at least 21 years of age and must be members of SCRABBLE Crossword Game Players, Inc.

3. Club Set Up

Owners may run their clubs for a profit or simply to cover expenses. Either way is fine. But, it is our official policy that the trademark not be used for any fund raising purpose. This means that the owner/director can make a profit or the money can be returned to the SCRABBLE PLAYERS Club for prizes, refreshments, etc. However, no proceeds from a SCRABBLE PLAYERS Club may be used for outside social causes or benefits.

4. Expert Points

SCRABBLE PLAYERS Clubs are open to everyone, but expert points are awarded exclusively to members of SCRABBLE Crossword Game Players.

Each time a SCRABBLE PLAYERS member wins a game, he/she will receive one black expert point. The more you win, the more black points you accumulate.

Do's and Don'ts for Clubs

- All SCRABBLE Crossword Game Clubs must be licensed by SCRABBLE PLAYERS.
- All prospective directors must take the certified director's test.
- All owners and directors must be at least 21 years old and members of SCRABBLE PLAYERS.
- The owner may run the club for a profit or simply to cover expenses.
- No charity fund raising or gambling allowed.
- The club may be open to the public or only to individuals in a certain organization.
- All are invited to play, but expert points are awarded exclusively to members of SCRABBLE PLAYERS.
- Clubs are licensed to run regularly scheduled sessions (i.e. weekly or semimonthly) at one location.
- No other activities (chess, checkers, backgammon, bridge, etc.) may be held in the same room during a licensed SCRABBLE PLAYERS Club session.

If you or your organization are interested in setting up a SCRABBLE PLAYERS Club, information is available by writing to SCRABBLE PLAYERS, 200 Fifth Avenue, New York, NY 10010.

D. By Mail/Solitaire SCRABBLE Crossword Game

SCRABBLE PLAYERS has received hundreds of requests for a system of SCRABBLE Crossword Game by Mail which people can play with distant friends and family members as a fun way to keep in touch. Now, By Mail/Solitaire SCRABBLE Crossword Game is available from SCRABBLE PLAYERS.

How does By Mail SCRABBLE Crossword Game work? This system involves two people: Player A and Player B. It consists of a sheet which is mailed back and forth between the players. Average length of a game runs anywhere from 12 to 20 turns apiece depending on your style of play.

This system also makes an enjoyable solitaire game for those people who would like to work on their games by themselves. A player can pit one hand against the other or play from one rack. Either way, it's enjoyable.

To receive By Mail/Solitaire SCRABBLE Crossword Game #1, send a check or money order in the amount of 75¢ to SCRABBLE PLAYERS, 200 Fifth Avenue, New York, NY 10010. Canadian Residents: Please send a postal money order in U.S. 75¢.

E. Film

"WHAT'S A SCRABBLE PLAYERS TOURNAMENT?"—13 minutes in color, 16mm sound—is a free loan film to groups. Your group pays return postage only.

This is a fast-moving, delightful film, shot during an actual SCRABBLE PLAYERS Tournament, sponsored by the New York City Department of Recreation. It captures people of all ages, from all walks of life: teachers, lawyers, truck drivers, students, secretaries, retirees, in the excitement of tournament play. The film also includes helpful hints on strategy from some of the players.

This film is available for group showings only. So, ask your group leader to schedule a showing date.

You can request it by sending the following information to: MODERN TALKING PICTURE SERVICE, 2323 New Hyde Park Road, New Hyde Park, NY 11040.

Group Leader's Name
Title
Name of Group or School
Address
City, State, Zip

Film Title: WHAT'S A SCRABBLE PLAYERS TOURNAMENT? #30722

Give a show date and an alternate date.
Be sure to order the film well in advance of the desired show date.

What Is A Trademark?

Chapter 2

A Trademark Is More Than a Name
A trademark is a company's fingerprint. An exclusive property and instant identity that makes it stand out from competition. SCRABBLE is our trademark. Owned by Selchow & Righter, alone. We regard it, proudly, as one of our most valuable assets. And it must be protected from all sides, at every level.

How Trademarks Get Lost in the Language
Unprotected trademarks simply disappear. Unfortunately, to reappear on someone else's products.

If a trademark is consistently misspelled, published as a generic term, commercially misused; if these abuses are not protested and followed by speedy legal action, the trademark may revert to public domain. Anyone can use it. And everyone will.

Take former trademarks like aspirin, escalator, and cellophane. Through misuse they have drifted into the language and onto imitators' labels.
On the other hand, properly protected trademarks remain the exclusive property of their owners. There is only one COCA-COLA Brand; one KODAK Brand; and one SCRABBLE Brand.

Keeping Our Trademark Intact
We watch it! SCRABBLE is always capitalized and is *never* the name of the game. The trademark SCRABBLE literally means: "Made by Selchow & Righter." Every time our SCRABBLE trademark is seen, it represents a reputation for quality and guarantees a standard of excellence. Therefore, it must be used exclusively to identify our goods and services. It cannot be associated with unauthorized organizations or tournaments. It should not share billing with money-making enterprises, no matter how charitable

their motives may be. And SCRABBLE is not a generic name description. Here are some of our SCRABBLE Brand games:

- RSVP Three Dimensional Crossword Game
- Crossword Game for Juniors
- Crossword Game
- Sentence Cubes
- Crossword Cubes
- Alphabet Game

The actual game names are Crossword Game, Crossword Cubes, and suchlike. SCRABBLE is their point of origin: their identification as established quality products. Our trademark.

Protecting Our Trademark
High visibility is the keynote. And our trademark must always stand out distinctively from surrounding copy. Examples:

> "Get everyone together with a SCRABBLE Crossword Game!"
> This is the right way
>
> "Get everyone together with a SCRABBLE Word Game!"
> This is acceptable.
>
> "Get everyone together for a game of SCRABBLE (or worse, scrabble)!"
> This is *wrong*.

The descriptive or generic name of our product should always follow the trademark. And our trademark must never be used to describe the game.

Perhaps innocently, and with the best intentions in the world, retailers, publications, and organizations may misuse our trademark. When this happens, the lapses should be immediately reported to our legal department. We, in turn, will point out the error of their ways. Nicely but firmly. It is a legality that is necessary to protect a trademark from sharing the fate of aspirin, escalator, and cellophane.

A Word About Copyrights
A copyright concerns literary and artistic expression. It represents the exclusive right to prevent unauthorized use or copying of what the United States Constitution terms "writing of authors." Rules, books, pamphlets, score sheets, and gameboards are copyrightable.

We Depend on You
By using our trademark correctly, you will be helping us. And we need your help. There are other word games and puzzles on the market—but only one SCRABBLE Brand. And, as we pointed out earlier, our trademark SCRABBLE is one of our most valuable possessions. Properly protected, it could last forever. With your cooperation, it will.

History Of Scrabble® Crossword Game

Chapter 3

What has 100 tiles . . . 225 squares . . . a multi-colored board . . . and millions of fans of all ages, backgrounds and locales?

The answer, of course, is SCRABBLE Crossword Game which took America by storm in the early 1950's—and has continued in popularity with game lovers since, not only in the United States but throughout the world.

James Brunot

How did the game come about? Who created it? And how did it catch the fancy of the public?

The story is as American as apple pie. In 1931 during the Depression, Alfred M. Butts, an out-of-work architect from Poughkeepsie, New York, decided to invent an adult board game. Analyzing all board games, he found they fell into three categories: number games, such as dice and bingo; move games, such as chess and checkers; and word games, such as anagrams. Mr. Butts, aiming for a game that would use both chance and skill, combined features of anagrams and the crossword puzzle —and called his new game Criss Cross.

Next he analyzed the English language. With 26 letters in our language, some letters are used more frequently than others. The one that does the most work is the letter "E". All the vowels appear far more often than do the consonants. He assigned different values to each letter. The letter "S" posed a problem. While it is used frequently, he concluded that only four "S's" should be included to avoid making the game too easy by the use of plurals.

The boards for his first Criss Cross game were hand drawn with his architectural drafting equipment, reproduced by blueprinting, and pasted on folding checker boards. The tiles were similarly hand lettered, then glued to ¼ inch plywood and cut to match the squares on the board.

While the game changed in its development (at one time the opening word was played near the upper left corner of the board), Mr. Butts at the outset chose a 15x15 symmetrical square pattern for the board, and designated seven as the number of tiles.

Many of the friends to whom Mr. Butts supplied handmade sample Criss Cross sets became enthusiastic devotees of his game. But the established game manufacturers to whom he submitted his invention were unanimous in rejecting it for commercial development. Mr. Butts, again busy as an architect, put aside his efforts to develop the game.

In 1948, Mr. and Mrs. James Brunot—who knew Alfred Butts, and had one of the original Criss Cross sets—thought the game should be marketed, so Mr. Butts authorized the Brunots to manufacture the game. They formed the Production and Marketing Company and set up shop in their Newtown, Connecticut home.

SCRABBLE
PLAYERS
OFFICIAL
TOURNAMENT

The first steps the Brunots took were to refine and improve the game. They rearranged the premium squares and completely revised the rules which had been long and complicated. One of their first concerns was protecting the game through a unique brand name that would qualify for registration as a trademark. The Brunots and their friends made up long lists of potential trademarks to be cleared by their law firm. Of all the brand names considered, SCRABBLE Brand came out with top honors and was cleared legally.

The Brunots rented a little abandoned schoolhouse in Dodgingtown, Connecticut where they and a friend turned out 12 games an hour, stamping letters one at a time on the wooden tiles. Later, boards, boxes, and tiles were made elsewhere and sent to the little factory for assembly and shipping.

The first four years were a struggle. Mr. Brunot kept his regular job. In

1949, the Brunots made 2,400 sets—and lost $450. But, year by year, the orders increased as news about the game got around, mainly by word of mouth. Then, in 1952, the Brunots left for a trip to Kentucky, and returned to find their little factory deluged with orders.

By 1953, it was obvious to the Brunots that they could no longer make the games themselves. They licensed Selchow & Righter Company, a well known game manufacturer founded in 1867, to market and distribute the games in the United States and Canada.

Even this company had to step up production to meet the overwhelming demand in the early Fifties. As stories about SCRABBLE Crossword Game appeared in national newspapers, magazines, and televison, it seemed that everybody had to have a set immediately. For three years, orders for the game had to be allocated so that customers received their fair share.

The game was no "fad". Rather, sales have gone steadily upwards, and today SCRABBLE Crossword Game is one of the leading board games in America, enjoying greater and greater popularity.

James Brunot remained active in developing a Braille set, working with the Connecticut State Board of Education for the Blind. He created for this set a revolving board with its own turntable to help the players . . . an innovation that was adapted for the SCRABBLE Crossword Game Deluxe set.

As well, Mr. Brunot worked with foreign language experts in developing five foreign language editions of the game—French, Spanish, Italian, German and Russian. He also worked with Selchow & Righter on the Magnetic Travel set, the DeLuxe set, and other SCRABBLE Brand games.

Scrabble® Players® Club & Tournament Rules

Chapter 4

SCRABBLE PLAYERS CLUB AND TOURNAMENT RULES

TO BEGIN

1. Count the tiles; there should be 100. Check the letter frequency with the list printed on the board. Place the tiles in the bag.

2. Each player draws from the bag for first play. The player drawing the letter nearest the beginning of the alphabet has first play. A blank tile supersedes all other tiles.

3. Both players return their draw tiles to the bag and the bag is shuffled thoroughly by either or both players.

START OFFICIAL CLOCK

4. The player with first play draws his seven tiles from the bag and places them on his rack. The opposing player repeats the process immediately. The initial player's three-minute timer is started and the game begins.

TIME

5. Official Clock—60 minutes.

a. Each game will run sixty (60) minutes and each player will be allowed three (3) minutes to put a completed word on the board.
b. The official clock marks the beginning and end of games for all players.
c. The Director will announce when six (6) minutes are left to play.
d. The official clock cannot be stopped for any problem that occurs in any individual game.

6. Individual Timers—3 minutes.

a. The turns of play will be timed by a three-minute timer. At the start of each player's turn, the timer must be set.
b. If a player completes his turn before the three minutes are up, he should return the timer to the start position, announce his score, and his opponent will start.
c. Each player must immediately notify his opponent if time has run out (three minutes) thereby preventing any additional tiles from being put into play.
d. Any player who has not placed a completed word on the board within the three-minute time limit loses his turn, and his opponent immediately begins his three minute turn.
e. The number of turns in a given game, depends upon the players' speed in forming words.

PLAY

7. The first player, should he choose to take his turn, combines two or more letters and places them on the board to form a word in either a horizontal or vertical position with one tile on the center pink square. The center pink square indicates double word score.

8. Diagonal words are not permitted.

9. Each time a turn is completed, the player counts and announces his score for that turn. He then draws as many new tiles as he has played, thus always keeping seven tiles in his rack.

10. In the meantime, his opponent adds one or more letters to those already played on the board and forms a new word or words. The horizontal and vertical positioning rule remains in effect during the entire game. Any words added to the board must touch words already formed and must make new words wherever they touch existing words or letters. The player gets credit for all words formed in this fashion.

11. New words may be formed by:

a. Adding one or more letters to a word already on the board.
b. Placing a word at right angles to a word already on the board. The new word must use one of the letters already on the board or must add a letter to it.
c. Placing a complete word parallel to a word already played, so that adjoining letters also form complete words.

12. Once a word has been placed on the board, a player may not shift the tiles. The Director is the final arbiter in all cases.

13. The two blank tiles may be used to represent any letter desired, but the letter it represents must be declared and the tile retains that designation throughout the game, and remains on the board.

14. Each time a blank is placed on the board, it is the responsibility of the opponent to turn the blank over to verify that it is truly a blank. If it is not a blank, the player who placed it on the board will take back his tiles and lose his turn. If a false blank is not detected when it is placed on the board, it will remain on the board as a blank and the game will continue with no penalty to either player.

15. *Whenever a player draws letters from the bag the procedure is as follows:*

> All tiles selected from the bag must be placed face down on the table beside the player's tile rack. The player will then verify that he has drawn the correct number of tiles for a total of seven (7). If he has drawn too many tiles, the excess tiles that he has just drawn will be removed by his opponent and replaced in the bag.

16. A player may use his turn to exchange letters in his rack for new letters. He does this by placing the desired number of letters from his rack on the table. He then selects the same number of tiles from the bag and places them face down on the table to verify that he has drawn the correct number of tiles. He then places the tiles he had wished to exchange into the bag and waits for his next turn.

17. A player may exchange tiles at any point in the game, provided there is a minimum of seven tiles remaining in the bag.

18. A player need not exchange tiles when passing; however, should both players pass three successive turns each, the game will be terminated.

19. The game proceeds until: 1) all the tiles are used; or 2) the Director announces the end of the game. Upon the Director's announcement, if a completed word is not on the board, no points will be given for that turn.

20. If a player has just finished placing a word on the board as the Director announces the end of the game, that player should replenish the 7 tiles in his rack (if enough tiles remain in the bag). Then the player should proceed with the end of game scoring.

21. At the end of each game, the Director will collect all of the score sheets and post the winner's name and score.

22. If a player must absent himself during the game, he will lose as many turns as it takes for him to return. A monitor will turn the absent player's three minute timer and the opponent will continue to play. The absent player will receive passes for those turns missed.

SCORING

23. The score value of each letter is indicated by a number at the bottom of the tile. The blanks have a score value of zero.

24. The score for each turn is the sum of the letter values in each word formed or modified during the play, plus the additional points obtained for placing letters on premium squares.

25. Premium letter squares:

a. A light blue square DOUBLES the score of a LETTER placed on it.
b. A dark blue square TRIPLES the score of a LETTER placed on it.

26. Premium word squares:

a. The score for an entire WORD is DOUBLED when one of its letters is placed on a pink square.
b. The score for an entire WORD is TRIPLED when one of its letters is placed on a red square.
c. When scoring a player's turn, all premiums for DOUBLE or TRIPLE letter values, if any, must be included before DOUBLING or TRIPLING the word score.

d. If a word is formed that covers two pink double word squares, the score is DOUBLED AND THEN REDOUBLED, which is FOUR times the total letter count.
e. If a word is formed that covers two red triple word score squares, the score is TRIPLED AND THEN RETRIPLED, which is NINE times the total letter count.
f. *The LETTER PREMIUMS and the WORD PREMIUMS apply only in the turn in which they are first played.* In all subsequent turns, letters count only at FACE VALUE.
g. When a BLANK TILE is played on a pink double word score square or a red triple word score square, the value of the word is DOUBLED or TRIPLED even though the blank tile, itself, has zero score value.

27. When two or more words are formed in the same play, each is fully scored. The COMMON LETTER IS COUNTED (with full premium value, if any) FOR EACH WORD.

28. Any player who plays ALL SEVEN of his tiles in a single turn, scores a premium of 50 points in addition to his regular score for the play.

29. (For club play, disregard paragraphs 7 through 10 and follow the instructions for use of the recorded score sheet). After each completed turn, a player announces his score before his opponent starts his turn, and fills it in on the score sheet. He then fills in the word or words formed on that play. At this point, the players verify each other's score by mutual consent. The scoring player then fills his rack with the appropriate number of tiles and his opponent starts his turn. At the end of each game the scores will be validated by the Director.

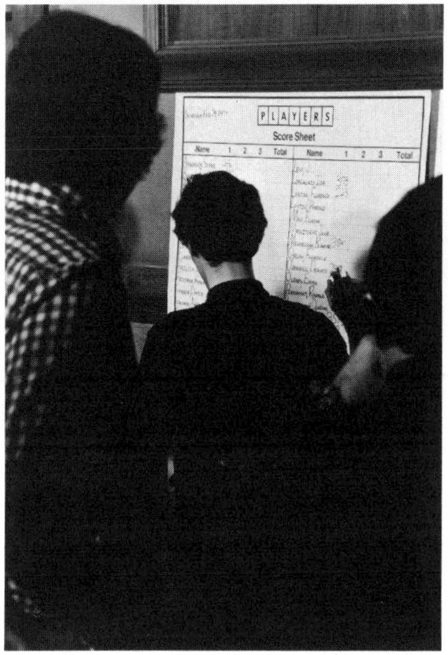
PLAYERS
Score Sheet

30. At the end of the game if both players have unplayed tiles left in their racks, each player's score is reduced by the sum of his unplayed letters. If, however, one player has used all his letters, his score is increased by *double* the sum of his opponent's unplayed letters and the opponent's score remains the same.

31. The player with the highest score wins the game.

32. In the event of a tie, the player with the highest single turn score will be declared the winner.

CHALLENGE

33. When a player completes his turn, his opponent may challenge any word or words that were formed on that play. If one of the words formed is unacceptable, the challenge is successful.

34. To challenge, a player must raise his hand and a monitor will come to his table.

35. If the challenged word is ruled unacceptable, the player who played it takes back the offensive tiles and loses his turn.

36. If the challenged word is acceptable, the word remains and the challenger loses his turn.

37. An unsuccessful challenger who loses his turn will enter pass on the score sheet for that turn.

38. The Director or his staff determine the validity of any challenged word.

DICTIONARY*

39. All words listed in the Funk & Wagnalls Standard College Dictionary, 1973-74 edition, *and labeled as a part of speech* (including those words designated as foreign, archaic, obsolete, colloquial, slang, alternate spellings) are permitted with the exception of the following: capitalized words, abbreviations, prefixes and suffixes standing alone, words requiring a hyphen or an apostrophe.

40. Words found in prefix sublists (un, non, re . . . etc.) which follow the above conditions, are acceptable although they are not listed as a part of speech.

41. The letters of the alphabet have a separate spelling and listing. For example: The letter "C" is spelled cee; pluralized it becomes cees. The letter "W" is spelled doubleyou. Pluralized it becomes doubleyous. CS and WS are not acceptable. Letters of foreign alphabets which have separate listings and are labeled as a part of speech are acceptable. Ex.: omega (n.). Foreign letters listed under the word "Alphabet" are not acceptable unless they are listed separately in the dictionary.

42. Funk & Wagnalls lists only the comparative (er) and the superlative (est) forms of one syllable adjectives where there is a spelling modification (i.e., dry, drier, driest) or a complete change of form (i.e., bad, worse, worst). Other comparative (er) and superlative (est) forms of one

*As soon as the SCRABBLE PLAYERS Dictionary is ready, it will be the official source for all SCRABBLE PLAYERS activities (see page 81).

syllable adjectives which don't require a spelling modification or a change of form and not found in Funk & Wagnalls will be acceptable, with the provision that they have a separate listing as an adjective or that the adjective definition is listed first (i.e., sweet [adj.]—sweeter, sweetest). Comparative (er) and superlative (est) forms of adjectives having two or more syllables must be listed in Funk & Wagnalls (i.e., happy, happier, happiest).

43. Funk & Wagnalls lists only the declension of verbs and the plurals of nouns in unusual situations (i.e., swim, swam, swum; man, men). Normal declensions and plurals will be accepted (i.e., talk, talking, talks, talked; boat, boats)

44. The dictionary cannot be consulted by any player nor is any other reading material whatsoever permitted throughout the course of the game. The Director and his staff are the only persons authorized to consult the dictionary. Any word used in the definition of a word but not listed in the dictionary itself, will not be acceptable.

45. If a word is not listed in the Funk & Wagnalls Standard College Dictionary, 1973-74 edition, or does not meet the above conditions or exceptions, it will be ruled unacceptable.

46. The Director will be the *final* arbiter in all instances and will rule *according to good English usage.*

Part 2

How To Use This Handbook

The SCRABBLE PLAYERS Handbook is written for all levels of SCRABBLE Crossword Game players. Some sections are very basic, while others expand into the realm of the expert player.

To illustrate the various points explained in the Handbook, each chapter has a number of diagrams. These diagrams do not represent the best possible plays, but rather, serve to highlight the particular point that is being discussed.

Through the use of these diagrams, the Handbook outlines the course of action in a great variety of game situations. Of course, each individual game is different so there can't be any "sure-fire" three easy steps to winning. However, a careful study of this Handbook, together with game practice will most definitely lead to game improvement.

Chapter 5

The Scrabble® Players® Notational System

It seems appropriate at this time to introduce the SCRABBLE PLAYERS Notational System which is used throughout the Handbook.

Each square of the SCRABBLE Crossword Game board has a unique identification. The horizontal columns are labeled A-O, going from left to right. The vertical columns are labeled 1-15, going from top to bottom. To identify any square on the board, the player gives the letter and number which intersect the square. For instance, in Diagram A, the horizontal word "WINTER" is notated: WINTER 8 D-I. All horizontal words are identified by a number and two letters.

The vertical word "SUMMERS" is notated: SUMMER[S] H 4-10. All vertical words are notated by one letter and two numbers.

In SUMMER[S], the letter E is underlined to show that it was already on the board, and the last S has a square around it to show that it's a blank.

The notation for RE is either 9 H-I or I 8-9.

Also included in this notational system is the rack of letters from which the play was made. This is essential to determine the merits of the play.
For example:

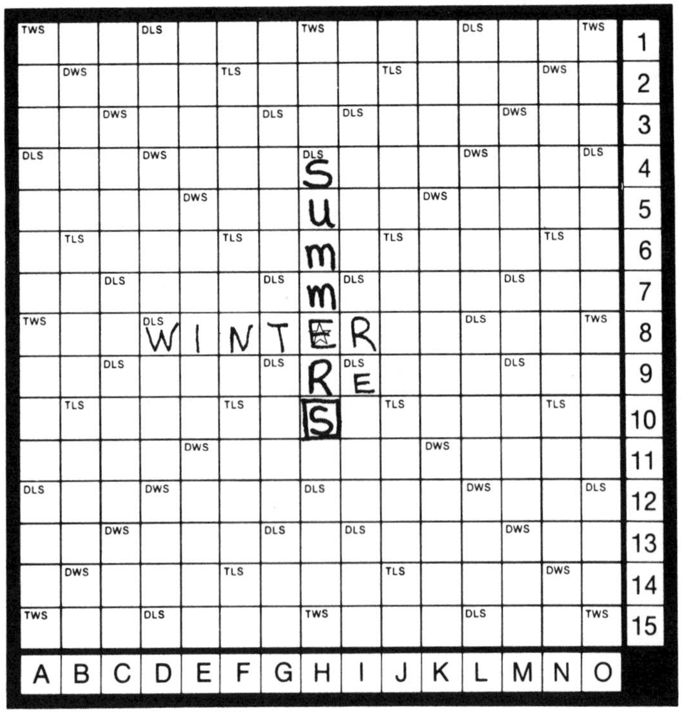
A B C D E F G H I J K L M N O
1 2 3 4 5 6 7 8 9 10 11 12 13 14 15
WINTER
SUMMERS
RE

DIAGRAM A

PLAYER A

Rack	Word	Play Notation
WINTERI	WINTER	8 D-I

PLAYER B

Rack	Word	Play Notation
SUMMR□R	SUMMER[S]	H 4-10

Thus, with the SCRABBLE PLAYERS Notational System, a player writes, 1) the rack, 2) the primary word played, and 3) the play notation to indicate where the word begins and ends on the board. All players should become familiar with this notational system, as it is used in the Handbook as well as in all SCRABBLE PLAYERS publications.

Levels Of Game Expertise

Chapter 6

A. Beginner

If you are new to SCRABBLE Crossword Game, there are certain areas of this Handbook which you should study carefully.

1) Familiarize yourself with the game board and its layout of premium squares. Then, become acquainted with the face value and frequency of the letters in the set (page 44). Make sure that you understand the SCRABBLE PLAYERS Notational System as described in Chapter 5.

2) Study Chapter 7 on Scoring very carefully. Concentrate on scoring the maximum points possible by using the premium squares and your high-valued tiles, as seen in Diagrams #7 and #8. Practice extending words already on the board by: 1) the use of inflected forms (Diagrams 1 and 2); and 2) the addition of letters before and after a word (Diagrams 3 and 4). Extending words such as RAP into GRAPES is a good technique to master.

3) Study the Questions & Answers: Playing Procedures beginning on page 37.

4) Develop your anagram skill. Practice looking for as many words as you can find in a random rack of seven letters. Set up your SCRABBLE Crossword Game board as in Diagram 20 on page 58. Don't look for words solely in your rack. Try to visualize the

letters of your rack in combination with letters already on the board. Given the rack SIAPDER how many possibilities can you find? Look for suffixes, prefixes, past tense forms, plurals, ER and EST. Try to find at least 30 possibilities. Concentrate on words of four, five, and six letters. Master these anagram and scoring techniques before trying to look for Bingos (see the Glossary for a definition of terms).

B. Average

If you are an average player, there are several areas that should be helpful.

1) Once you have mastered the Beginner techniques mentioned in Section A, go on to study other sections of Chapter 7 on Scoring. Concentrate on forming more than one word as in Diagrams 3, 4, 5, 6, 9, 10, 11, and 12.

2) Expand your scoring techniques by consciously creating good rack leaves for Bingo opportunities (see the Glossary for a definition of terms). Study Chapter 8 on Tile Distribution and Chapter 11 on Anagrams. Remember that Bingos should not hinder your game, but add to it. It does you no good to sit with Bingo tiles in your rack, if you cannot mentally rearrange the letters to find the Bingo. Strive to expand your anagram skill to find the Bingos in your rack in conjunction with the tiles on the board. Look at Quiz Diagram 10 on page 150. Without checking the answer, how many Bingos can you find with the rack NTOLIIA in conjunction with the Quiz Diagram?

3) Be sure to learn your two and three-letter words (Part 8). These are the means of linking letters to words already on the board to form Bingos.

C. Above Average

If you are a better than average player, then you have already mastered Sections A and B, in addition to Chapter 7. Make sure that the two and three-letters words are under your belt (Part 8). Concentrate on the defensive and offensive characteristics of letters of the alphabet (Chapter 9) and the strategy through the various sections of the game (Chapters 12, 13, and 14). Consider the Handbook as an overview; take in the subtleties: Bluffs and Challenges (Chapter 16) and Various Styles of Play (Chapter 17). Pay special attention to the game section which highlights all the topics discussed in the Handbook.

D. Questions & Answers: Playing Procedures

Here are questions that many players ask.

1. May a Dictionary Be Consulted Before Placing a Word on the Board?

No. A dictionary may be consulted only *after* a word has been placed on the board and challenged. If you were playing with a child, then it would be better to look up words before they were placed on the board. This would then be a fun way to learn about words, the dictionary, etc.

2. Is There a Limit to the Number of Times a Certain Word May Be Used During the Course of a Game?

No. If players wish to use the word "it" several times during a game, this is acceptable.

3. If the Player Who Goes First Wishes to Pass, Does the Next Player Receive the Double Word Score for Covering the Center Star?

Yes. Any player who covers the premium square receives that premium value.

4. What About Passing at the End of the Game?

At the end of the game, players may pass their turn just as they can in the opening or middle moves. However, if *each* player passes three times in a row, the game ends. In the Club and Tournament rules, a player may exchange letters right up until there are seven tiles remaining in the pool. After that, a player may pass his turn but may not exchange tiles.

5. How Does the Game End?

There are two possible endings to SCRABBLE Crossword Game.

1. The game ends when there are no tiles in the pool and one player has used all his tiles. Although the other players have tiles remaining in their racks, they cannot put them on the board as the game is over. The player who played all his tiles receives the value of the unplayed tiles remaining in the other players' racks. The other players subtract the value of their unplayed tiles from their own scores. This is called "the end of game scoring." For club and tournament "end of game scoring," see page 27.

or

2. The game ends when there are no tiles in the pool and each player has a few remaining tiles but no place to put them on the board. In this case, each player subtracts the value of the unplayed tiles in his rack from his own score.

6. Can a Player Form More Than One Word During a Single Turn?

During one turn in SCRABBLE Crossword Game, the tiles are placed in *one* row to form one primary word. If, in placing these tiles in one row, they touch other tiles on the board, they may form several secondary words at the same time. The player receives credit for *all* words formed or modified (i.e. adding an S or an R to a word already on the board, etc.) during that turn. See Diagram B, turn #2A, #2 B, #3B.

7. Once a Tile Covers a Premium Square, May the Next Player Recount the Value of that Premium Square if He Adds an "S" to the Word?

No. The premium squares (double or triple letter; double or triple word) apply only in the turn in which they are first played. See turn #1A and #1B.

8. What About Premium Values if Two Words Are Formed?

When two or more words are formed in the same play, each is scored. The common letter is counted (with full premium value) in the score of each word. See turn #2A.

9. What Happens When You Cover Two Triple Word Squares in One Turn?

One triple word score is three times the value of the entire word. Two triple word scores equal nine times the value of the entire word. See turn #3A. One double word score is two times the value of the entire word; and two double word scores equal four times the value of the entire word.

10. If a Player Places a 7-Letter Word on a Premium Word Square, Is the 50-Point Bonus Doubled or Tripled?

No. The value of the word is doubled or tripled, then the 50-point bonus is added. See turn #3A.

11. If a Player Adds an "S" to a Word Already on the Board, Is This Considered Forming a New Word?

Yes. If Player A put the word HORSE on the board, it is perfectly acceptable for Player B to add an S to make HORSES. The same is true if Player A put the verb TALK on the board; Player B could add ING or ED or S, and receive credit for the entire word.

12. If a Word Is Already on the Board, Can a Player Add Letters Before and After It During a Single Turn to Form Another Word?

Yes. If the word RAP is on the board, a player may add a "G" in front and "ES" at the end to form GRAPES. This constitutes one turn, as the letters are placed in one row to form one primary word. See turn #1A and #1B.

13. What Happens When a Blank Is Placed on a Double or Triple Word Square?

When a blank is placed on a double or triple *word* square, the player gets double or triple the value of the word. If at the same time, the blank adds a letter to a word already on the board, the player gets double or triple the value of that *word*, too. Of course, a blank on a double or triple *letter* score is of no value as the blank has no point count. See turn #2B.

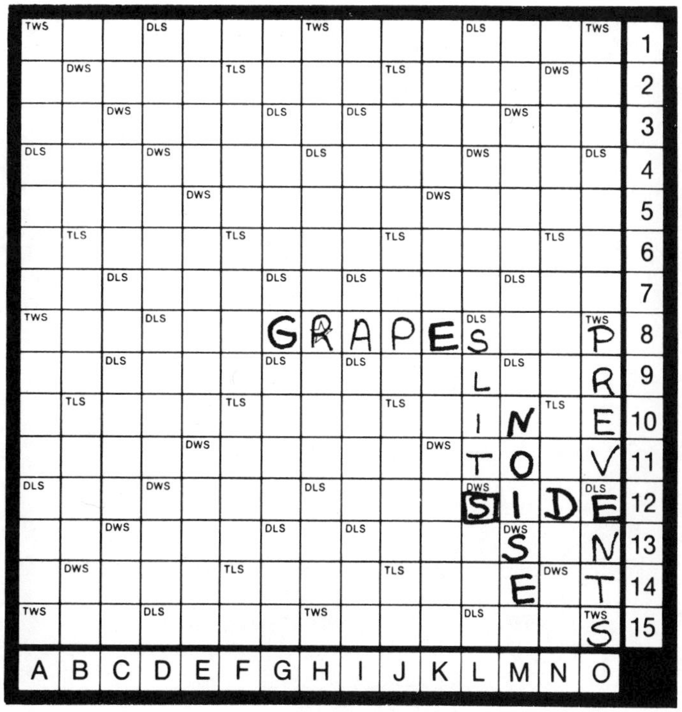

GRAPES
SLIT
SIDE
NOISE
PREVENTS
A B C D E F G H I J K L M N O
1 2 3 4 5 6 7 8 9 10 11 12 13 14 15

DIAGRAM B

PLAYER A

	Rack	Word	Play Notation	Score
#1A.	RAPLITN	RAP	8 H-J	10 pts.

RAP = 5 pts. × DWS = 10 pts.

	Rack	Word	Play Notation	Score
#2A.	LITNSTS	SLIT	L 8-11	15 pts.

SLIT = 5 pts.; GRAPES = 10 pts.
S = DLS for each word

	Rack	Word	Play Notation	Score
#3A.	NTSPREV	PREVENTS	O 8-15	167 pts.

PREVENTS = 13 pts. × 9 (2 TWS) = 117 pts.
Bonus for all 7 tiles 50
167 pts.

PLAYER B

	Rack	Word	Play Notation	Score
#1B.	GEIDNOE	GRAPE	8 G-K	8 pts.

Adding letters before and after a word already on the board.

	Rack	Word	Play Notation	Score
#2B.	IDNOEE□	[S]IDE	12 L-O	18 pts.

[S]IDE = 5 pts. × DWS = 10 pts.
SLIT[S] =4 pts. × DWS = 8 pts.

	Rack	Word	Play Notation	Score
#3B.	NOESITE	NOISE	M 10-14	14 pts.

NOISE = 5 pts. × DWS = 10 pts.
IN = 2 pts.; TO = 2 pts.

DWS = Double Word Score DLS = Double Letter Score TWS = Triple Word Score

14. Once a Blank Is on the Board, Can It Be Exchanged for the Letter It Represents?

No. Once a blank is placed on the board, it remains on the board throughout the entire game.

15. Does the Second Blank Have to Represent the Same Letter as the First Blank?

No. If the first blank represents a "K", it must remain on the board as a "K" throughout that game. The second blank, however, need not represent a "K"; it could be a "D", but it, too, must remain on the board as a "D" throughout that game .

16. Who Is the Winner of the Game?

The winner of SCRABBLE Crossword Game is the player with the highest score after the end of game scoring.

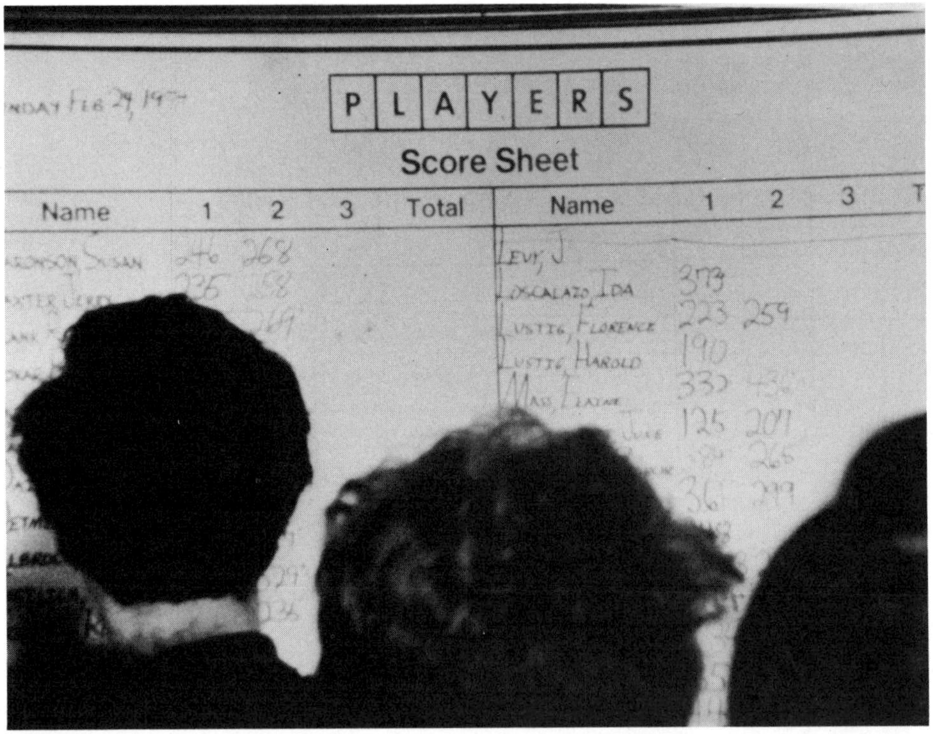
P L A Y E R S
Score Sheet
Name 1 2 3 Total
Name 1 2 3

Part 3

Tactics

The player who sees no other aim in SCRABBLE Crossword Game than to score the maximum number of points, will never be a good player. It is useless to score 400 points a turn if an opponent will, as a consequence of that play, score considerably more. Therefore, the skilled SCRABBLE Crossword Game player resembles a boxer more than a slugger. He constantly maneuvers for advantage and concedes as little as possible to his opponent. Before a good player can do this, he must know the basics of the game.

Therefore, a careful examination of scoring methods will be discussed. Only after summarizing these basic scoring elements will the discussion move on to the more advanced strategy and tactics of the game.

Chapter 7

Scoring

Before learning the elements of strategy that SCRABBLE Crossword Game encompasses, it is necessary to be totally familiar with all the methods of scoring high-point plays during a single turn. Scoring is possible in many ways:

1. Extending words already on the board.
2. The use of high-valued tiles.
3. The use of premium squares (double or triple letter squares/double or triple word squares).
4. The use of Bingos (seven letter bonus words for an extra 50 points).
5. A combination of 1, 2, 3, and 4.

This chapter will be a systematic presentation of these scoring methods. Players should follow these examples carefully, as they are closely linked to the strategic concepts discussed later in the book.

First, a summary of the individual letters of the alphabet, their face value and frequency in the set:

Letter	Face Value	No. in Set
A	1	9
B	3	2
C	3	2
D	2	4
E	1	12
F	4	2
G	2	3
H	4	2
I	1	9
J	8	1
K	5	1
L	1	4
M	3	2
N	1	6
O	1	8
P	3	2
Q	10	1
R	1	6
S	1	4
T	1	6
U	1	4
V	4	2
W	4	2
X	8	1
Y	4	2
Z	10	1
Blank	0	2

A. Extending Words Already On The Board

A common method of scoring is to extend words which are already on the board. This may be done in three ways:

1. The use of plurals.
2. The use of all other inflected forms of words; declensions, comparatives, etc.
3. Creating new words by adding letters either before or after words already played on the board.

1. The Use of Plurals

The use of plurals is one of the most common methods of scoring. In Diagram 1, Player A has the rack CINPSWZ and plays ZINCS, I 4-8 to make ZINCS and QUAFFS for a total of 40 points. Player B has the rack AGHSVVY and plays SAVVY 13 F-J to make JACKALS and SAVVY for a total of 39 points.*

DIAGRAM 1

PLAYER A

Rack	Word	Play Notation	Score
CINPSWZ	ZINCS	I 4-8	40

PLAYER B

Rack	Word	Play Notation	Score
AGHSVVY	SAVVY	13 F-J	39

1
2
3
4
5
6
7
8
9
10
11
12
13
14
15
A B C D E F G H I J K L M N O
ZINCS
QUAFFS
JACKALS
SAVVY

Fortunately, such opportunities abound in the game since a player gets not only the value of the new word but also the value of the word already on the board.

*Player A erred in not pluralizing JACKAL with ZINCS for 52 points.

2. The Use of Other Inflected Forms

Another method of extending words already played is by adding endings such as *er*, *est*, *ing*, *es*, etc. For instance, in Diagram 2, Player A adds ED to QUAFF, 8 D-J for 23 points, while Player B adds ER to BLACK F 6-12 for 15 points. Each player used an inflected form to score. This method of scoring is not used particularly frequently as the point count is rather low.

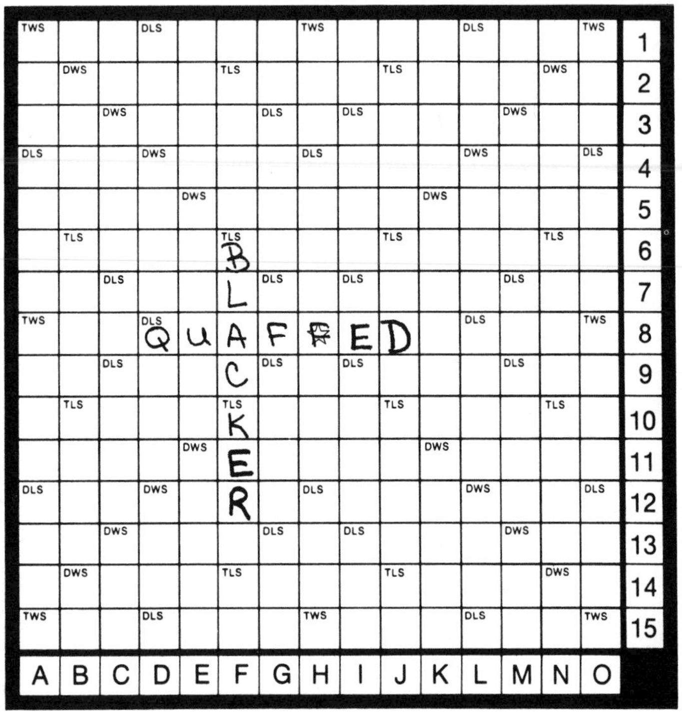

DIAGRAM 2

PLAYER A

Rack	Word	Play Notation	Score
DEEMRTX	QUAFFED	8 D-J	23

PLAYER B

Rack	Word	Play Notation	Score
EEEGRRV	BLACKER	F 6-12	15

3. Creating New Words by Using Tiles Already Played

A much more frequent method of scoring is to add letters either before or after tiles that are already on the board to create new words. These opportunities occur regularly during a game. For instance, in Diagram 3 Player A has the tiles ZINCLIW and scores 40 points by expanding the

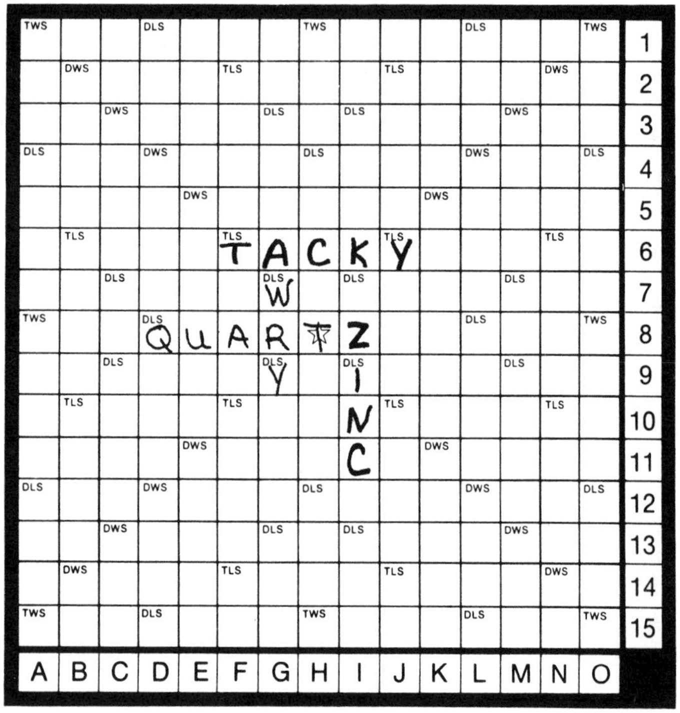

DIAGRAM 3

PLAYER A

Rack	Word	Play Notation	Score
ZINCLIW	ZINC	I 8-11	40

PLAYER B

Rack	Word	Play Notation	Score
ATCKYVS	TACKY	6 F-J	34

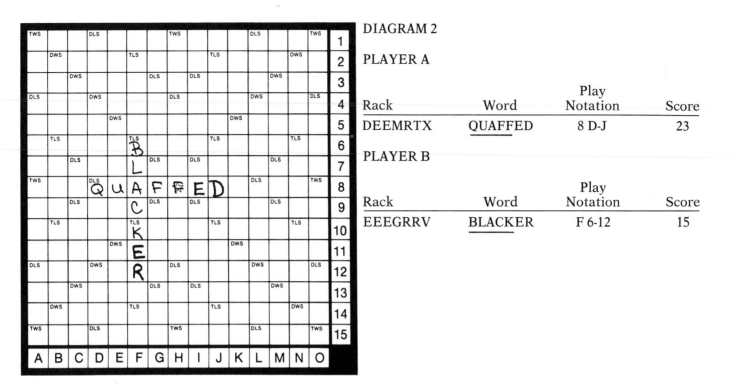

already existing word QUART into QUARTZ, with the play ZINC, I 8-11. Similarly, Player B has the tiles ATCKYVS and expands the word WRY into AWRY for 34 points with the play TACKY, 6 F-J.

This method of scoring is so simple, yet effective, that every serious player should know how to use it. Diagram 4 illustrates two more examples of this theme. Player A with the tiles BRAZENW expands STAMPED to STAMPEDE, and scores 41 points with the play BRAZEN, M 4-9. Player B with the tiles FLOWNGR extends LUMMOX into FLUMMOX, and scores a neat 43 points with the play FLOWN, D 10-14.

DIAGRAM 4

PLAYER A

Rack	Word	Play Notation	Score
BRAZENW	BRAZEN	M 4-9	41

PLAYER B

Rack	Word	Play Notation	Score
FLOWNGR	FLOWN	D 10-14	43

STAMPEDE
FLUMMOX
BRAZEN
FLOWN

A much more common and useful means of scoring is playing on top of, underneath, and alongside existing words to create a group of new words. The player completing such a play gets the points for every new word created. In Diagram 5 Player A uses the letters from DONATOR 8 D-J, by playing GONAD, 7 E-I, directly on top of it. He thus, creates five additional words (GO, ON, NA, AT, DO) plus GONAD for a total of 25 points.

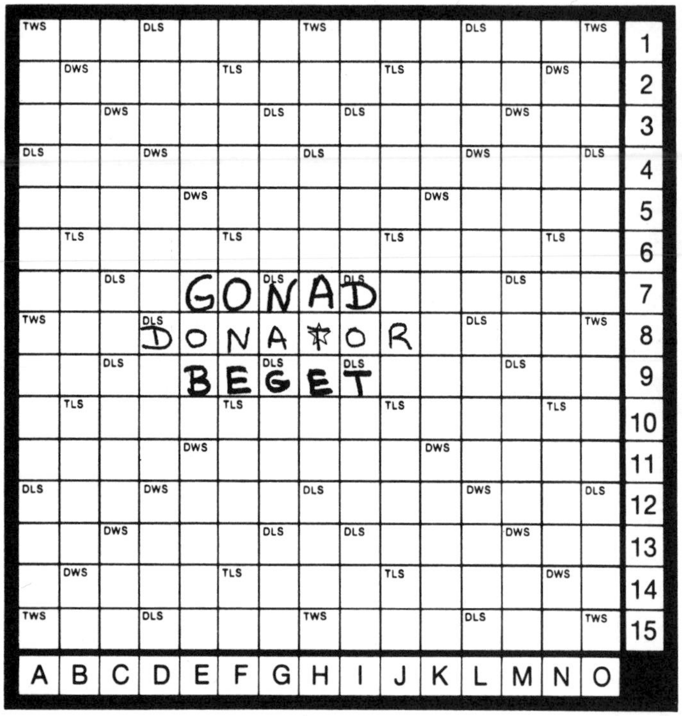
GONAD
DONATOR
BEGET

DIAGRAM 5

PLAYER A

Rack	Word	Play Notation	Score
AGGDNOC	GONAD	7 E-I	25

PLAYER B

Rack	Word	Play Notation	Score
BEEGHST	BEGET	9 E-I	34

Player B responds by playing under DONATOR, the word BEGET, 9 E-I, for 34 points. Note that Player B's play was worth more points since the series of words he created included Player A's letters from the previous play (GOB, ONE, NAG, ATE, DOT).

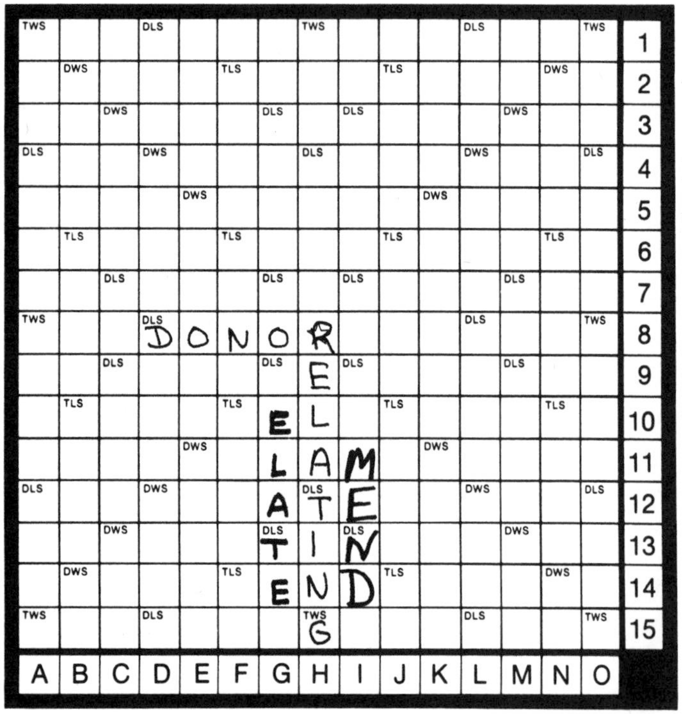
DONOR
RELATING
ELATE
LAM
MEND
END
ATE
TIN

DIAGRAM 6

PLAYER A

Rack	Word	Play Notation	Score
AEELQTU	ELATE	G 10-14	17

PLAYER B

Rack	Word	Play Notation	Score
DEOJMNV	MEND	I 11-14	24

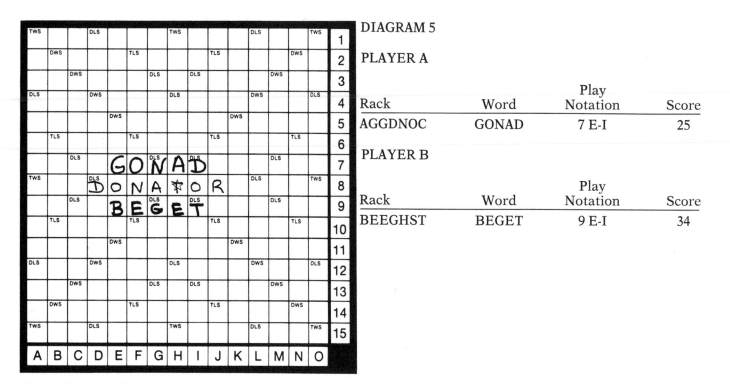

Diagram 6 illustrates the principle of playing alongside vertical words. Player A plays ELATE G 10-14, alongside RELATING, H 8-15 for 17 points. Player B responds with MEND, I 11-14 for 24 points.

B. Using High-Valued Tiles

The simplest method of scoring is to use the high-valued tiles. In Diagram 7, Player A scores 20 points by playing QUACK, H 7-11. Player B counterscores by playing QUIZ 7 H-K for 23 points.

DIAGRAM 7

PLAYER A

Rack	Word	Play Notation	Score
ACDGKQU	QUACK	H 7-11	20

PLAYER B

Rack	Word	Play Notation	Score
BILSEUZ	QUIZ	7 H-K	23

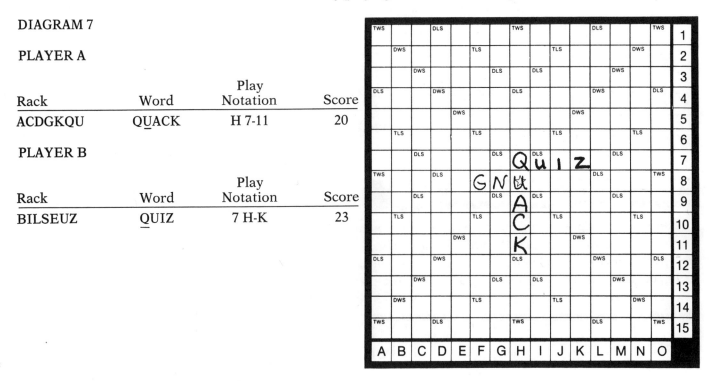

Even though each player scored in the 20's, these scores aren't high enough to merit the use of so many high-valued tiles in a single turn.

A much more effective means of scoring is by placing high-valued tiles on the premium squares of the board.

1. Double and Triple Letter Squares

In Diagram 8, Player A scores 32 points with the play FLANK 8 D-H. Notice he places the letter F on the double letter square scoring double the value for that letter. Player B responds with the play ZEAL F 6-9 getting three times the value for his Z by placing it on the triple letter square.

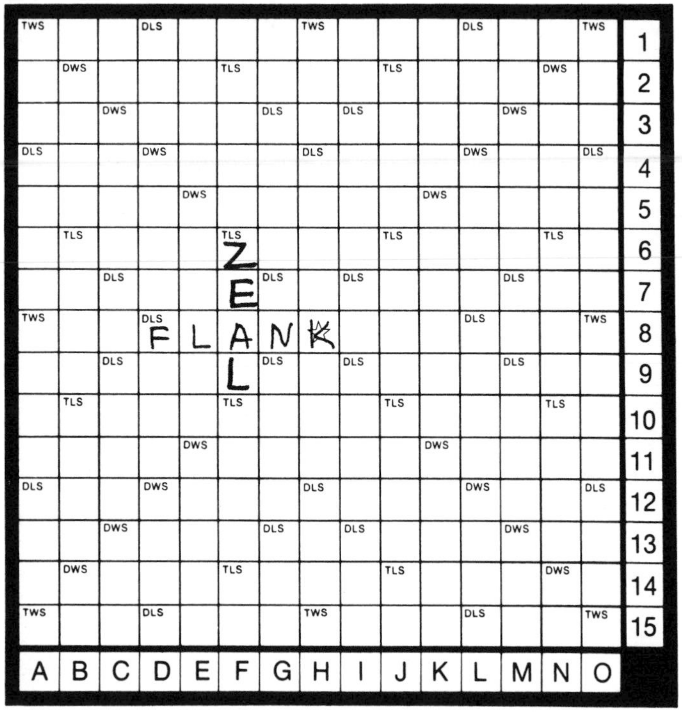

DIAGRAM 8

PLAYER A

Rack	Word	Play Notation	Score
ALNKFRO	FLANK	8 D-H	32

PLAYER B

Rack	Word	Play Notation	Score
ZLEBMIR	ZEAL	F 6-9	33

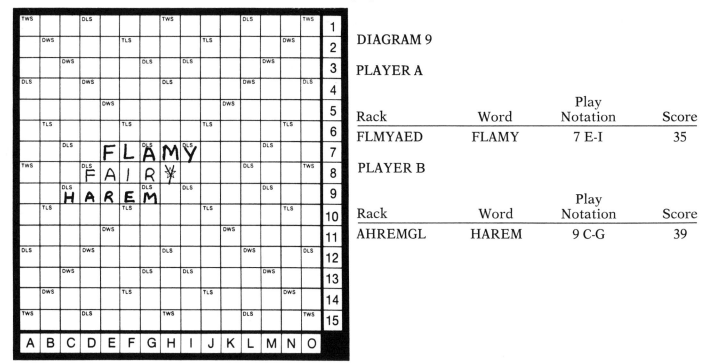

The double and triple letter squares may be used even more effectively by placing high-valued letters on the double and triple letter squares so that the letters quadruple in point count. In Diagram 9, Player A makes ordinary use of the double letter squares with the play FLAMY 7 E-I for 35 points. Player B, however, scores 39 points with the play HAREM

DIAGRAM 9

PLAYER A

Rack	Word	Play Notation	Score
FLMYAED	FLAMY	7 E-I	35

PLAYER B

Rack	Word	Play Notation	Score
AHREMGL	HAREM	9 C-G	39

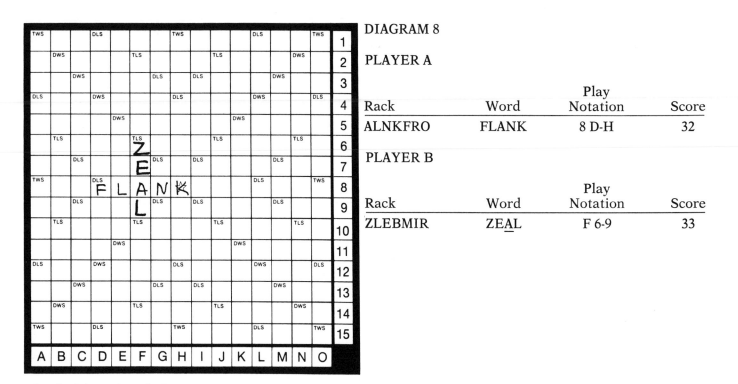

9 C-G. Notice he gets 12 points for his M, quadrupling its actual face value (six points for the M in HAREM and another six for the M in ARM G 7-9).

In Diagram 10, Player A plays the word TAXED 9 E-I for 51 points, 32 of which are for placing the X on the double letter square (16 points for the X in TAXED and 16 for the X in EX, G 8-9). Player B responds with the word OHO 7 F-H for 38 points, 16 of which are derived from placing the H on the double letter square. In each case the players received four times the value of the tiles played.

DIAGRAM 10

PLAYER A

Rack	Word	Play Notation	Score
AXEDTRL	TAXED	9 E-I	51

PLAYER B

Rack	Word	Play Notation	Score
OOHEDLS	OHO	7 F-H	38

OHO
BAKED
TAXED

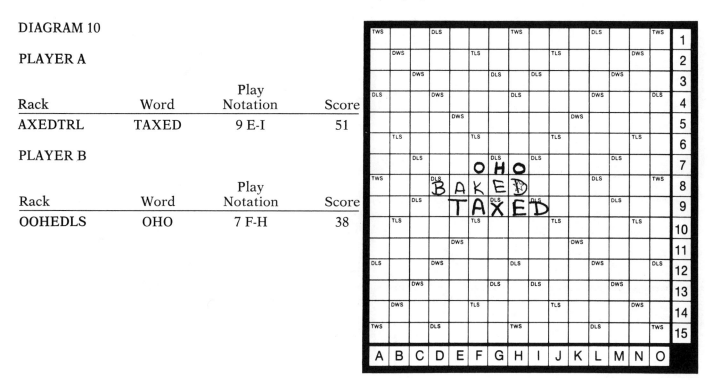

Triple letter squares may be used in a way that the player may get six times the face value of his tile. Diagram 11 shows Player A making the play ZEST 10 F-I for 66 points, 60 of which are for the Z. Player B plays YOUNG J 10-14 for 46 points, 24 of which are for the Y.

HEAVED
WAND
ZESTY
YOUNG

DIAGRAM 11

PLAYER A

Rack	Word	Play Notation	Score
ZESTSLM	ZEST	10 F-I	66

PLAYER B

Rack	Word	Play Notation	Score
YOUNGRT	YOUNG	J 10-14	46

Two other common examples of high scores by using the triple letter squares are illustrated in Diagram 12. Player A neatly uses his X on the triple letter square with the word FOX J 4-6 for 59 points. Player B counters with the play JAR F 6-8 for 53 points. Both players secured 48 points for their high-valued tiles.

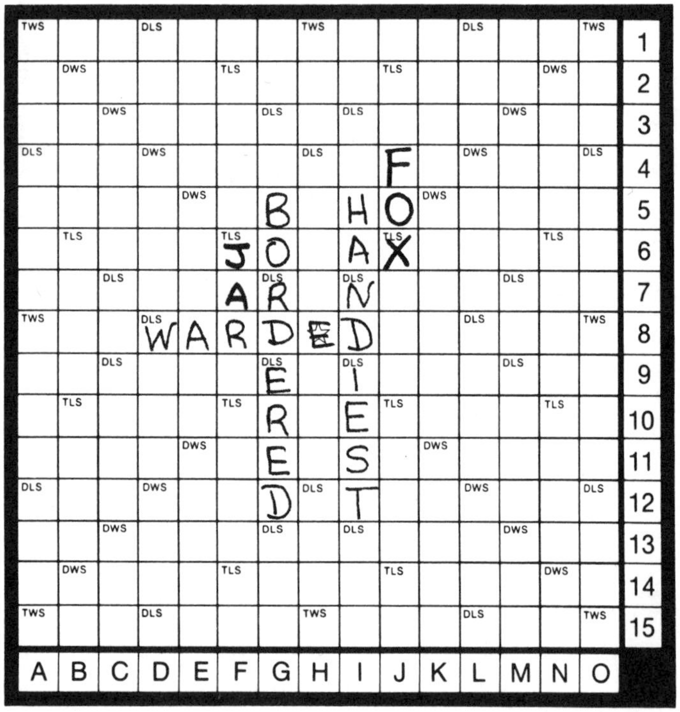
FOX
HOAX
JAR
BOARDERED
WARDED
HANDIEST

DIAGRAM 12

PLAYER A

Rack	Word	Play Notation	Score
XOFYMAE	FOX	J 4-6	59

PLAYER B

Rack	Word	Play Notation	Score
JATIRES	JAR	F 6-8	53

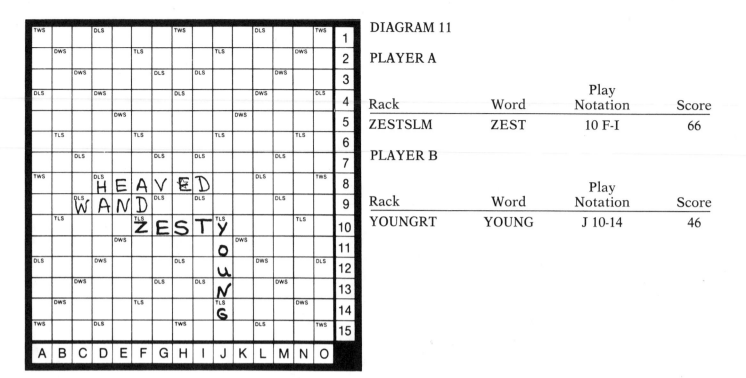

2. Double and Triple Word Squares

More valuable than the double and triple letter squares (with the possible exception of getting 4 or 6 times the face value of a high-valued tile) are the double and triple word squares. This is because only one letter of the word has to be placed on the premium word square in order to double or triple the value of the *entire* word.

Diagram 13 shows two common examples of the use of double word squares. Player A plays WAXY 8 H-K for 34 points and Player B responds with FLAKY K 4-8 for 30 points.

DIAGRAM 13

PLAYER A

Rack	Word	Play Notation	Score
WAXYJTO	WAXY	8 H-K	34

PLAYER B

Rack	Word	Play Notation	Score
FLAKRTE	FLAKY	K 4-8	30

FLAKY
WAXY

Naturally triple word squares are more valuable than double word squares. Two examples of their use are given in Diagram 14. Player A makes the word CANNY 1 F-J for 30 points. Player B replies strongly with the word DARKENS O 9-15 for 51 points.

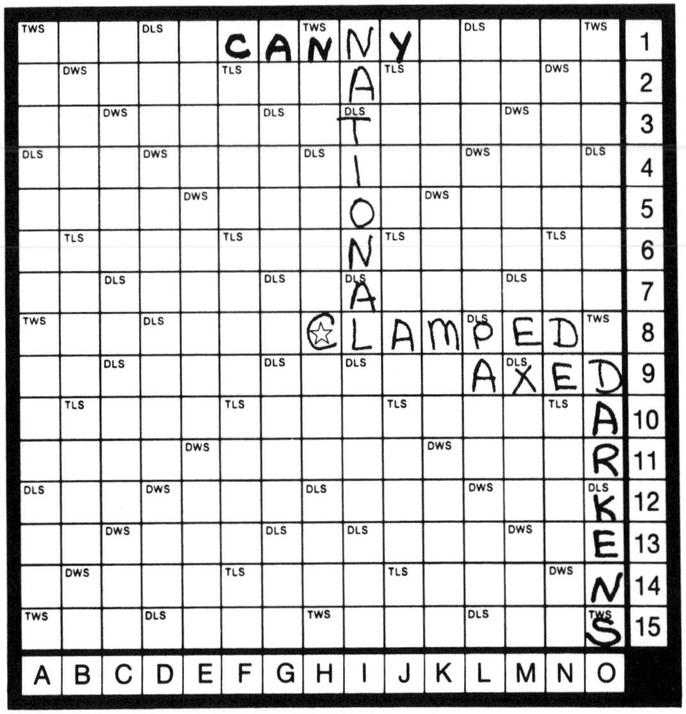

DIAGRAM 14

PLAYER A

Rack	Word	Play Notation	Score
CANYELB	CANNY	1 F-J	30

PLAYER B

Rack	Word	Play Notation	Score
ARKENSG	DARKENS	O 9-15	51

Player B's play also illustrates the use of the premium letter squares in combination with the premium word squares. He plays the high-valued tile K on a double letter square (O-12) and extends the word DARKENS into the triple word square O-15.

Diagrams 15 to 17 illustrate common examples of this theme.

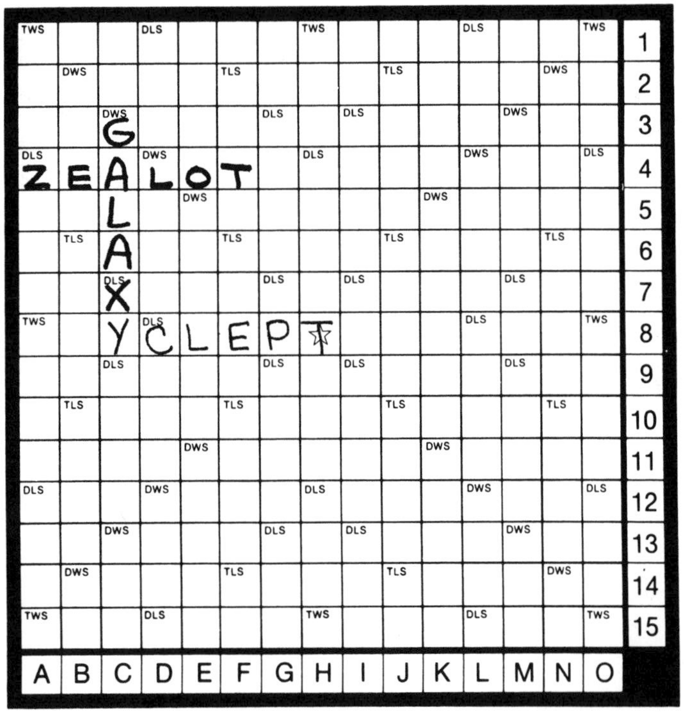

DIAGRAM 15

PLAYER A

Rack	Word	Play Notation	Score
GALAXAL	GALAXY	C 3-8	50

PLAYER B

Rack	Word	Play Notation	Score
ZELOTRN	ZEALOT	4 A-F	50

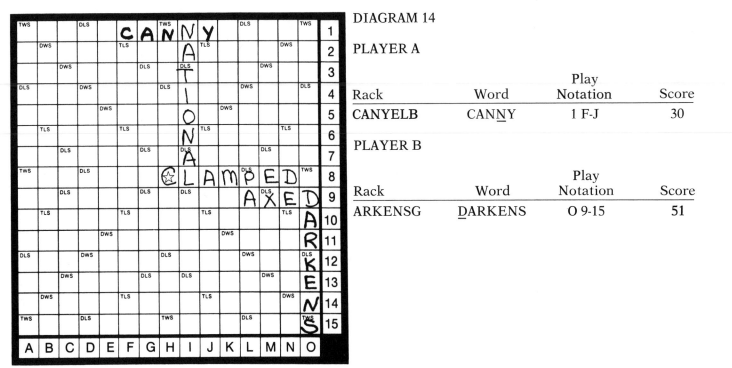

Player A gets 50 points in Diagram 15 by placing his X on the double letter square C-7 and extending his play to the double word square C-3 to make GALAXY C 3-8. Player B acts similarly with the play ZEALOT 4 A-F for 50 points.

Player A in Diagram 16 gets 6 times the value of his J by playing JOCKEY 2 J-O for 76 points. Player B makes a similar play with the word QUEER N 10-14 for 68 points.

DIAGRAM 16

PLAYER A

Rack	Word	Play Notation	Score
JOKEYRA	JOCKEY	2 J-O	76

PLAYER B

Rack	Word	Play Notation	Score
QUERARF	QUEER	N 10-14	68

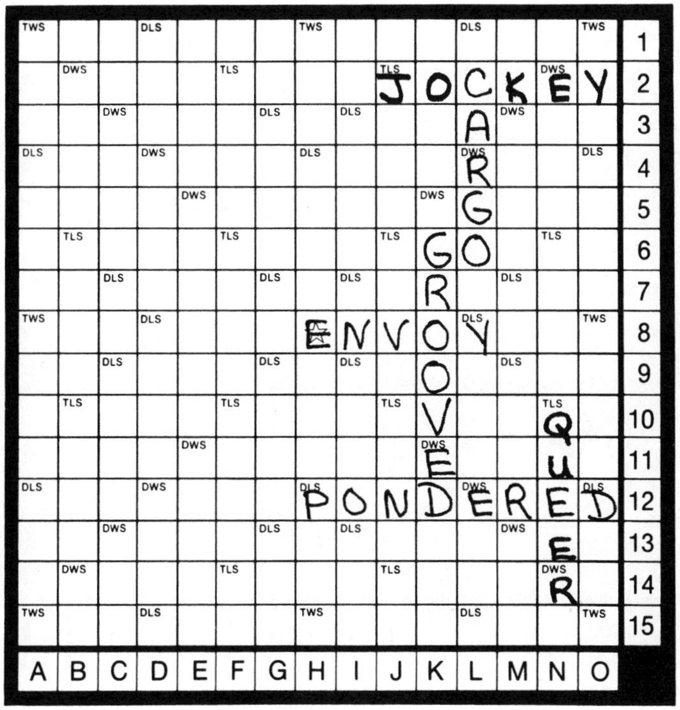

JOCKEY
CARGO
GROOVE
ENVOY
PONDERED
QUEER

Diagram 17 illustrates how the triple word squares in combination with double letter squares combine for very high scoring plays. Player A plays INTAKE 15 H-M for 45 points. Notice, he gets 6 times the value of his K. Player B, however, responds with a tremendous score of 116 points with the play WOOZY A 1-5. Here he gets 8 times the value of his Z, six times for the word WOOZY and twice more for creating the new word ZAMIA, 4 A-E.

DIAGRAM 17

PLAYER A

Rack	Word	Play Notation	Score
ITAKEYS	INTAKE	15 H-M	45

PLAYER B

Rack	Word	Play Notation	Score
WOOZYER	WOOZY	A 1-5	116

3. Two Double and Triple Word Squares

Another tactic that has not yet been discussed is the use of two double and triple word squares on one play. When this occurs the player gets four or nine times the value of his play.

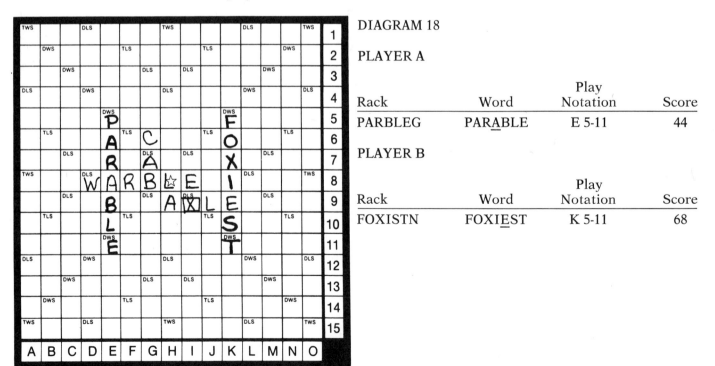

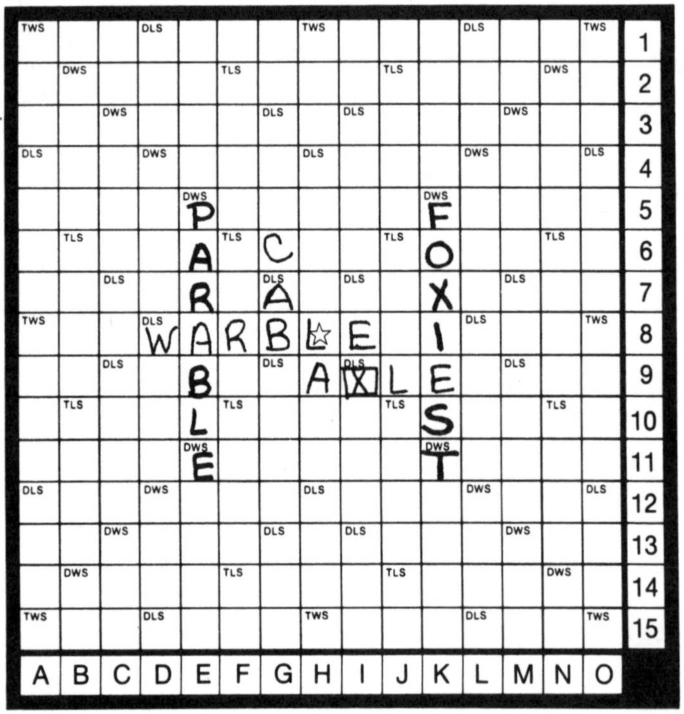

DIAGRAM 18

PLAYER A

Rack	Word	Play Notation	Score
PARBLEG	PARABLE	E 5-11	44

PLAYER B

Rack	Word	Play Notation	Score
FOXISTN	FOXIEST	K 5-11	68

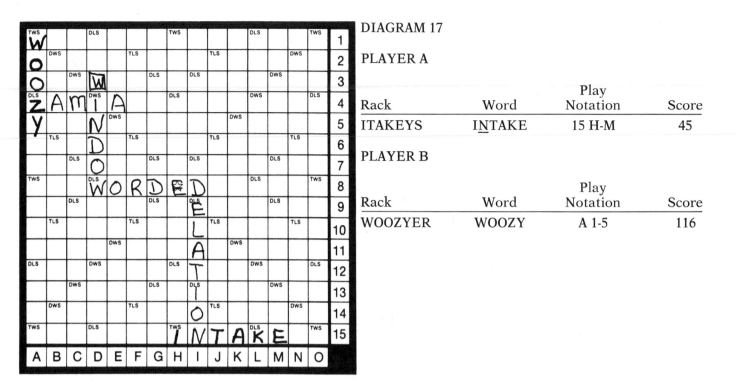

Two excellent double-double word plays are shown in Diagram 18. Player A neatly uses two double word squares with the word PARABLE E 5-11 for 44 points. Player B counters with FOXIEST K 5-11 for 68 points.

Triple-Triple scores rarely occur in play (except in the case of Bingos) but nevertheless must be shown because of their exceptional high point count. In Diagram 19, Player A employs two triple word squares with the play STRETCHY O 8-15 for 144 points. Player B also uses two triples with CREEPING 1 H-O for 117 points.

DIAGRAM 19

PLAYER A

Rack	Word	Play Notation	Score
STYAOIR	STRETCHY	O 8-15	144

PLAYER B

Rack	Word	Play Notation	Score
CREENGT	CREEPING	1 H-O	117

CREEPING
PARKA
IDEA
PETERED
HAREM
JESTER
STRETCHY
A B C D E F G H I J K L M N O
1 2 3 4 5 6 7 8 9 10 11 12 13 14 15

C. Bingos

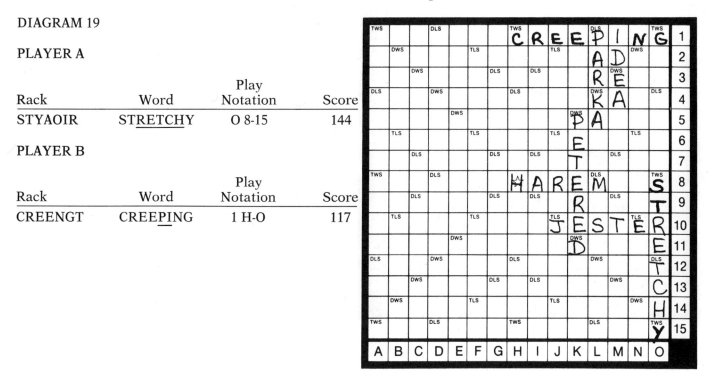

In the previous examples there were three basic themes:

1) Extending and building on words already played
2) The use of high-valued tiles
3) The use of the premium squares

These three themes increase in difficulty as they are combined in any one play.

A player receives a 50 point bonus for playing away all seven of his tiles in one turn. This rule enables a player with low-valued tiles to score a high point play.

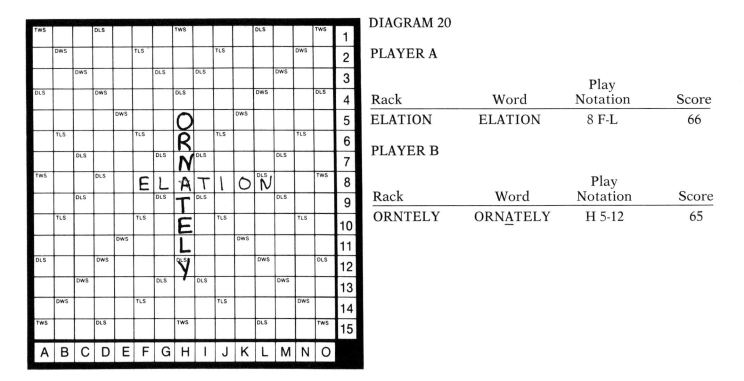

In Diagram 20, Player A plays ELATION 8 F-L for 16 points plus the 50 point bonus for a total of 66 points. Player B plays ORNATELY H 5-12 for 15 points plus the bonus for a total of 65 points. Notice that Player B's word is longer than A's because he uses one of A's letters for his own play. The requirement for a Bingo is that a player use all seven of his tiles on any one play. Thus, a Bingo may be anywhere from 7 to 15 letters in length.

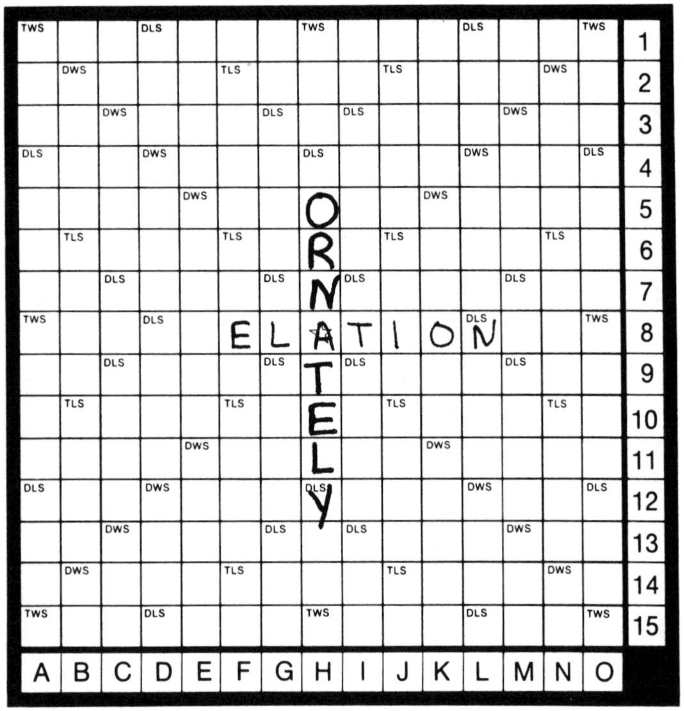
ELATION
ORNATELY
1 2 3 4 5 6 7 8 9 10 11 12 13 14 15
A B C D E F G H I J K L M N O

DIAGRAM 20

PLAYER A

Rack	Word	Play Notation	Score
ELATION	ELATION	8 F-L	66

PLAYER B

Rack	Word	Play Notation	Score
ORNTELY	ORNATELY	H 5-12	65

When a Bingo combines with a normally high scoring play, extraordinarily high scores are achieved. In Diagram 21, both players begin the game with Bingos. Player A gets 116 points for SQUAWKS 8 C-I and Player B gets 146 points for HIGHJACK H 1-8.

DIAGRAM 21

PLAYER A

Rack	Word	Play Notation	Score
SQUAWKS	SQUAWKS	8 C-I	116

PLAYER B

Rack	Word	Play Notation	Score
HIGHJAC	HIGHJACK	H 1-8	146

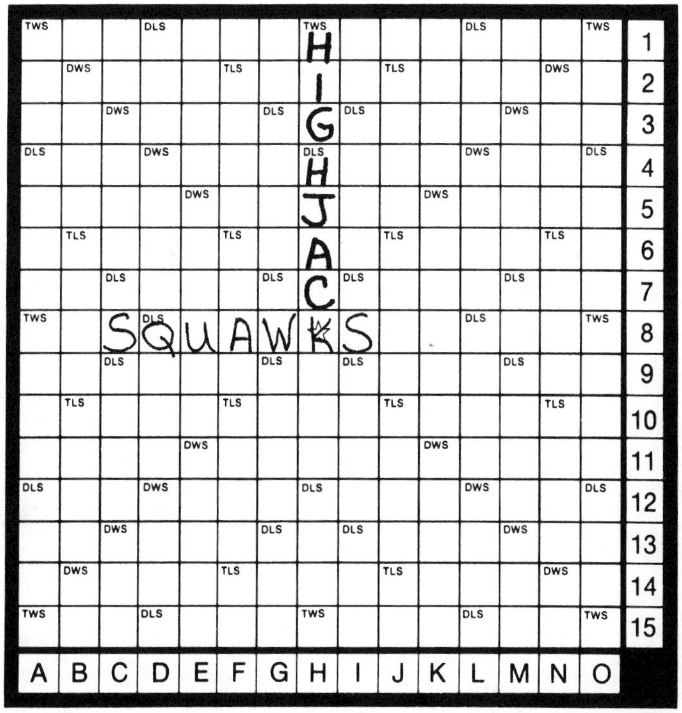

HIGHJACK
SQUAWKS

In Diagram 22 Player A gets 120 points for the fine Bingo MAJESTIC B 8-15, while Player B gets 164 points for the equally fine counterplay CAZIQUES 15 B-I.

DIAGRAM 22

PLAYER A

Rack	Word	Play Notation	Score
MJESTIC	MAJESTIC	B 8-15	120

PLAYER B

Rack	Word	Play Notation	Score
AZIQUES	CAZIQUES	15 B-I	164

PANDA
WAXED
MAJESTIC
CAZIQUES

Two final types of Bingo plays are double-double and triple-triple words. These scores, plus the 50 point bonus, make enormous scores possible.

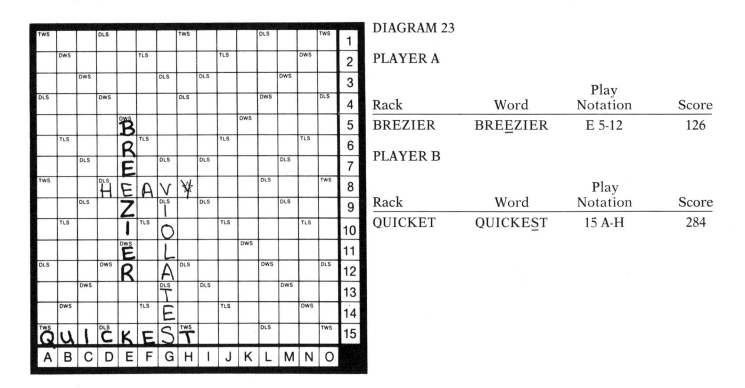

In Diagram 23 player A scores 126 points with the play BREEZIER E 5-12. Player B, however, scores a triple-triple Bingo with the word QUICKEST 15 A-H for 284 points!

This last play rarely occurs but is so decisive when it is played that it must be in every player's repertoire. Triple-triple Bingos may go as high as 360 points!

BREEZIER
HEAVY
VIOLATES
QUICKEST

DIAGRAM 23

PLAYER A

Rack	Word	Play Notation	Score
BREZIER	BREEZIER	E 5-12	126

PLAYER B

Rack	Word	Play Notation	Score
QUICKET	QUICKEST	15 A-H	284

The tips contained in this chapter can add a great many points to any player's score. But it's not enough just to know the basic elements of scoring. A player must also learn how to manipulate his tiles. Therefore, the discussion will now turn to the importance of tile distribution.

Tile Distribution

Chapter 8

A. Balancing The Rack

Crucial to a player's general success is tile distribution. A player should make every effort to play a word which has not only a good point count, but also leaves good tiles in his rack for his next turn. This chapter will cover rack development for plays leaving three to five tiles in the rack.

The key words here are flexibility and balance—flexibility so that a player can profitably use any tiles he draws on his next turn. In order to do this, a player must balance his leave. Leave refers to the tiles left in the rack after a player's turn; and balance refers to the number of vowels and consonants in the rack.

Ideally, a player should have an equal number of vowels and consonants remaining in his rack after a play. If he leaves himself without any vowels (or consonants, as the case may be), a player may find that he is unable to form a word on his next turn. Too many vowels or consonants leave a player unable to do any constructive scoring or defending.

N I R

For example, the letters POMPNEL are in a player's rack. Assuming that he has an option on this play, it would be better for him to leave at least one vowel in his rack. Playing POMP would be better than playing MOPE, as the latter play leaves three consonants in the rack. If, however, the player did play MOPE and did not draw a vowel on his next turn, he would probably have to pass.

Conversely, if a player has the tiles IOAUELN, he should make every effort to play away a majority of the vowels—in particular, UOI, which leaves the tiles LANE in his rack. This is rack development.

B. Duplication

A situation worse than imbalance in a player's rack, is duplication. This refers to having two or more of the same letter in the rack and will inevitably lead to a loss of turn in the future.

For instance, a player has the tiles ALLINEI. This combination is not good, as there are two L's and two I's in the seven letters. Therefore, a player must try to keep a balanced leave and at the same time play away one L and one I.

Avoiding duplication is a constant battle. Whenever a player picks a tile which is a duplicate, he must plan ahead in order to eliminate the duplication on his next turn. Many people hold the misconception that two O's or two L's in a rack are easily played away and look for words with these combinations. This, however, limits play to strict word forms which make up only a small percentage of the language . . . not to mention, what happens if a player draws a third O or L. Since duplication of letters will occur naturally during the game, a player should not hunt for these combinations.

C. Tile Management

If the player has learned the value of keeping a balanced rack, and the importance of avoiding duplication, he must learn which tiles to keep in his rack. Tile management has the general aim of developing a rack towards the greatest Bingo possibilities.

Bingo tiles are determined by two general factors. 1) Their frequency in the set (there are nine A's, twelve E's, six R's, etc.) and 2) the number of other letters they will combine with to form Bingos.

Nine tiles come up frequently in Bingo racks. They are: AEISTRNGD. Experience has shown that six of these letters in various combinations are the most Bingo prone—SATIRE. Eighteen letters of the alphabet combine with SATIRE to produce Bingos.

A—Aristae
B—Baiters, Terbias, Barites
C—Raciest, Stearic
D—Tirades, Staider, Astride, Diaster, Disrate
E—Seriate
F—Fairest
G—Stagier, Gaiters, Seagirt, Aigrets
H—Hastier
I—Airiest
J—None
K—None
L—Retails, Slatier, Realist, Saltire, Saltier
M—Imarets, Misrate
N—Retains, Stainer, Nastier, Ratines, Retinas, Stearin
O—None
P—Parties, Traipse, Pastier, Pirates, Piaster
Q—None
R—Tarries, Tarsier
S—Satires
T—Ratites, Tastier, Artiste, Striate, Attires
U—None
V—Vastier, Veritas
W—Wariest, Waiters, Wastrie
X—None
Y—None
Z—None

Another letter combination which is Bingo prone is RETINA. This, together with seventeen letters of the alphabet, produce Bingos. But RETINA does not combine with another A.

A—None
B—None
C—Certain, Creatin
D—Trained, Detrain
E—Trainee, Retinae
F—Fainter
G—Granite, Ingrate, Tangier, Tearing
H—Inearth
I—Inertia
J—None
K—Keratin, Intaker
L—Latrine, Ratline, Retinal, Reliant, Trenail
M—Minaret, Raiment
N—Entrain
O—None
P—Pertain, Painter, Repaint
Q—None
R—Terrain, Trainer, Retrain
S—Stearin, Stainer, Nastier, Retinas, Retains, Ratines
T—Nitrate, Tertian, Nattier
U—Taurine, Ruinate, Urinate, Uranite
V—None
W—Tinware, Tawnier
X—None
Y—None
Z—None

D. Sacrificing Point Count

The discussion of rack development is on an ideal plane. A player is looking for flexibility through a balanced rack, avoiding duplication, and building his rack towards a Bingo combination. Often the sacrifice of points on a particular play is preferable to playing away these tiles and losing flexibility. For instance, in Diagram 1, Player A has the letters AENIITH. He plays CHINA 5 D-H for 20 points rather than ETH K 5-7 for 25 points. CHINA leaves him with TIE in his rack, whereas ETH leaves him with AIIN. To maintain a flexible rack, CHINA is a preferable play although the point count is five points less. These points will easily be made up on the next play.

DIAGRAM 1

Rack	Word	Play Notation	Score
AENIITH	CHINA	5 D-H	20
Rather than	ETH	K 5-7	25

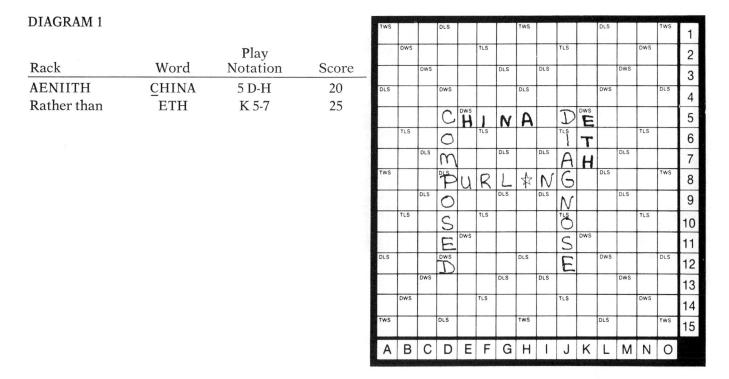

Many such opportunities for keeping a balanced rack occur during the course of a game and should not be neglected for a high point score. Similarly, it is often worthwhile for a player to risk a large play by his opponent in order to maintain tile flexibility.

For instance, in Diagram 2 Player A has the tiles INIONES. He can play INION 10 B-F for 15 points, which leaves ES in his rack. Although his opponent could add M to make MINION and play through the triple word square at 15-A, experience has shown that in the long run Player A will gain more than he loses.

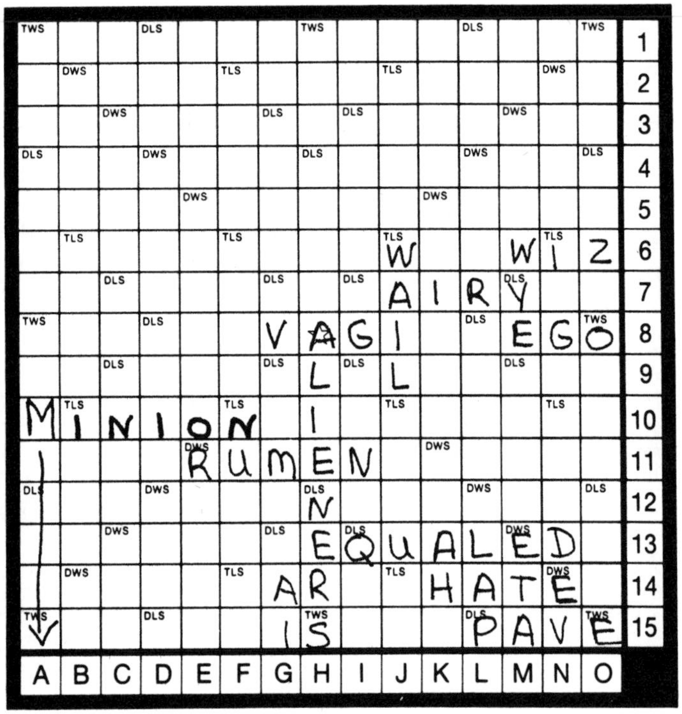

DIAGRAM 2

Rack	Word	Play Notation	Score
INIONES	INION	10 B-F	15

E. Passing

There is another method of tile management which often becomes necessary and that is passing. Provided there are at least seven tiles remaining in the set, a player has the option of passing some or all of his tiles. As a rule, a player should pass only to rid himself of completely unmanageable tiles. This is the device used when the normal method of tile flexibility does not succeed.

For instance, a player has the rack AEEEIUR. It is extremely unlikely that he would be able to play away enough tiles to balance his rack. Consequently, passing is necessary. The player should pass all seven tiles as it would be quite likely that he would duplicate letters if he did not exchange them all. Not passing all seven tiles diminishes a player's chances of picking up a high-valued tile, blank, or S that remains in the set. As a general rule, when a player passes to achieve tile flexibility, he should pass all seven tiles.

Exception: Do not pass S's or blank tiles.

F. Fishing

Fishing is the term used in reference to looking for a particular letter. Generally speaking, it is bad strategy. There is one instance, however, in which it may pay off. If a player has SATIRE or RETINA or a combination extremely close to this, it often pays to pass one or two tiles that are not a part of the combination with the hopes of picking up one of the many Bingo tiles. This is not considered passing for rack development, since the rack is already well-developed towards a Bingo possibility. Passing at this time is a calculated risk that a player takes in order to play a Bingo on his next turn.

Tile distribution is crucial to a player's success, but it's an area that a great many players overlook. All players interested in game improvement are urged to study this chapter and then practice the principles described.

Hand in hand with tile distribution are the tools of SCRABBLE Crossword Game—the letters of the alphabet. Discussion will now move on to an analysis of the vowels, consonants, blanks, and the special case of the Q and the U.

KENT

Chapter 9

The Letters

Every gamesman should be familiar with the tools of his game. In the case of SCRABBLE Crossword Game, the tools are:

- the letters that create the plays
- the frequency of the individual letters in the set (see page 44)
- the value of the letters
- the premium squares on the board which can double or triple the value of the words formed.

A. The Vowels

The vowels A, E, I, O, U, are an interesting group of letters. The value of any particular vowel depends on how well it combines with other letters. E and A combine with more letters than any other vowel and are better able to sustain duplication.

I, O, U combine with fewer letters than do E and A, and are not as good in developing a player's rack towards Bingo possibilities. The U must be carefully watched so that it can be matched up with the Q, particularly in the later stages of the game (see Part C of this Chapter).

I, O, U are not as able to sustain duplication. It is much easier to play away two A's or two E's than it is two I's, two O's or two U's. Although many words have double O's, drawing a third O would be definitely cumbersome. Therefore, players should not hunt for duplication as it will occur naturally during the course of a game. (see Chapter 8-B, DUPLICATION).

In balancing his rack, a player should give preference to the vowels in this order: E, A, I, O, U. Good vowel combinations to keep are: EA, AI, IE. Weak combinations are: IU, AU, AO.

B. The Consonants

The consonants are broken down into several catagories:

1) Defensive tiles—C, V
2) Intermediate tiles—D, L, N, R, T
3) Offensive tiles—F, H, M, P, Y
4) Semi-Defensive/Semi-Offensive tiles—G, K, B
5) High-Valued tiles—J, Q, X, Z
6) Most Valuable tiles—S, Blank

1. Defensive Tiles

Defensive tiles such as C and V are often used as a means of blocking Bingos and preventing an opponent from making high point plays. As we have seen, most Bingos are formed by chaining the bonus word to the board by means of a two-letter word. There are no two-letter words beginning or ending with C or V. The same is true of Q and Z, but they are such high-valued tiles that they are usually used offensively.

C and V, as well as many other consonants, can be used to block premium squares. If Player A places a consonant next to a premium letter square, Player B will not be able to use that square for high point count. Why? Because Player B will be forced to place either a vowel or a low-valued consonant on that premium square.

2. Intermediate Tiles

The intermediate tiles are D, L, N, R, T. Their point value is low but they combine well with many vowels to form Bingo possibilities. These consonants play a key role in developing a Bingo rack.

3. Offensive Tiles

The offensive tiles F, H, M, P, Y (valued three to four points apiece) are good for Bingo development, as well as for high point count on premium squares. More often than not when a Bingo is not immediate, these tiles are placed on the premium squares to make a small play with a high point count.

4. Semi-Defensive/Semi-Offensive Tiles

The semi-defensive/semi-offensive tiles are G, K, B. They are semi-defensive in that there are no two-letter words ending in these consonants. They are semi-offensive in that they can be played on premium squares for a good point count.

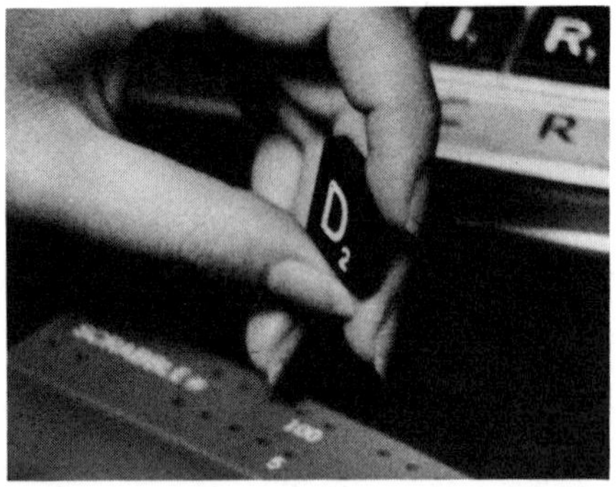

5. High-Valued Tiles

The high-valued tiles are J, Q, X, Z. The easiest tile to play is the X, as it combines well with other tiles for Bingo possibilities and is a good letter for premium squares. J and Z are not as flexible in combining with other Bingo-prone tiles, while the Q is the least valuable of the four.

It is a good idea not to hold on to these high-valued tiles too long. If a player draws another high-valued tile, his rack becomes cumbersome and he loses a great deal of flexibility.

6. Most Valuable Tiles

The most valuable tiles in the SCRABBLE Crossword Game set are the S's and Blanks. The Blanks are thoroughly discussed in Part D of this Chapter, so this passage will deal with S's. The S is the most frequent and versatile letter in our language. It has a great many high-valued Bingo possibilities. Offensively it can be added to almost any high-point word on the board for a good score; defensively it can be added to nouns and verbs so that an opponent can add nothing more to these words.

S's should not be wasted. A player should count the number already on the board and play his S only on a profitable play (this holds true in the case of duplication, too). If it is necessary for a player to pass his tiles, he should keep the S as it is one of the few tiles that goes well with duplication.

7. Consonant Combinations

Letter combinations are an important part of the game. Just as certain vowels combine well together, so do certain consonants: GHT, CH, WH, PH. One combination to avoid in a seven-letter rack is WU. If this combination occurs, play away the W or the U as quickly as possible.

C. The Q & The U

The Q is the least valuable of the high-valued tiles. As its face value is 10 points, it is often used in plays of high point count. However, the Q is useless without a U; this often makes its value negative rather than positive.

The Q without a U handcuffs a player's Bingo possibilities and makes rack improvement very difficult; in essence, a player is playing with only six tiles.

Good players keep on eye out for the Q until it has been placed on the board. This calls for definite "Q-strategy" during the various stages of the game.

1. Opening Game Q-Strategy

In the opening stages of the game, it is often a good idea to pass the Q in order to play for a bonus word. For example, in Diagram 1, Player A has the tiles QSATIRE. In this case he would definitely pass the Q as it is probable that he would draw one of the 18 letters that combine with SATIRE to form a Bingo.

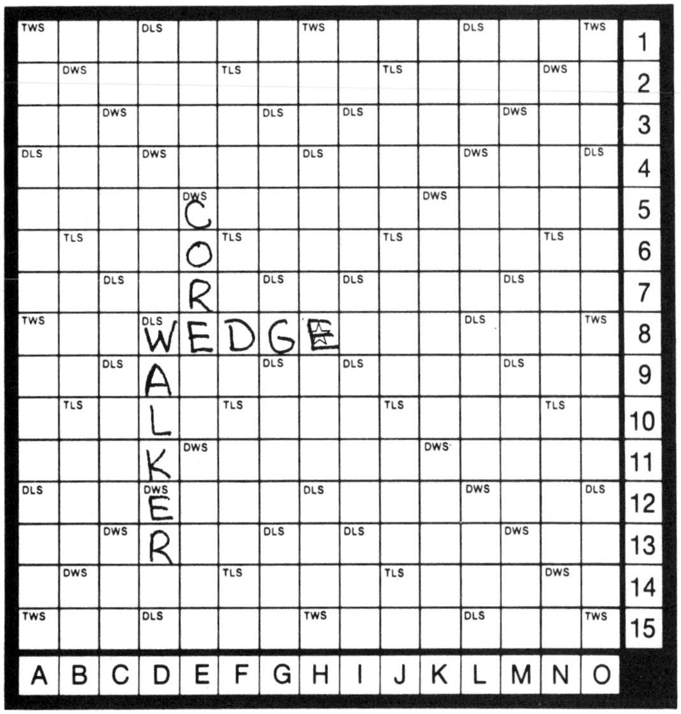

DIAGRAM 1

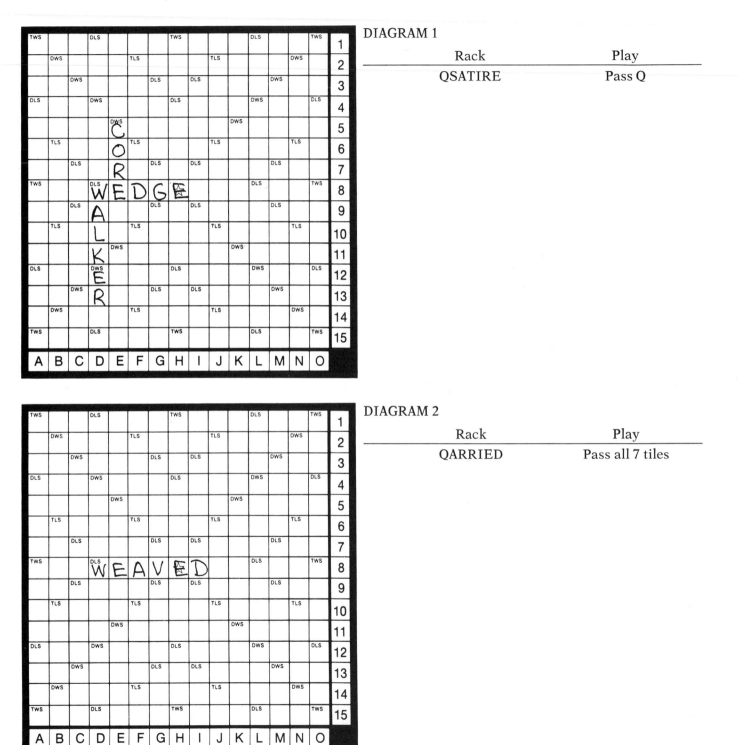

Rack	Play
QSATIRE	Pass Q

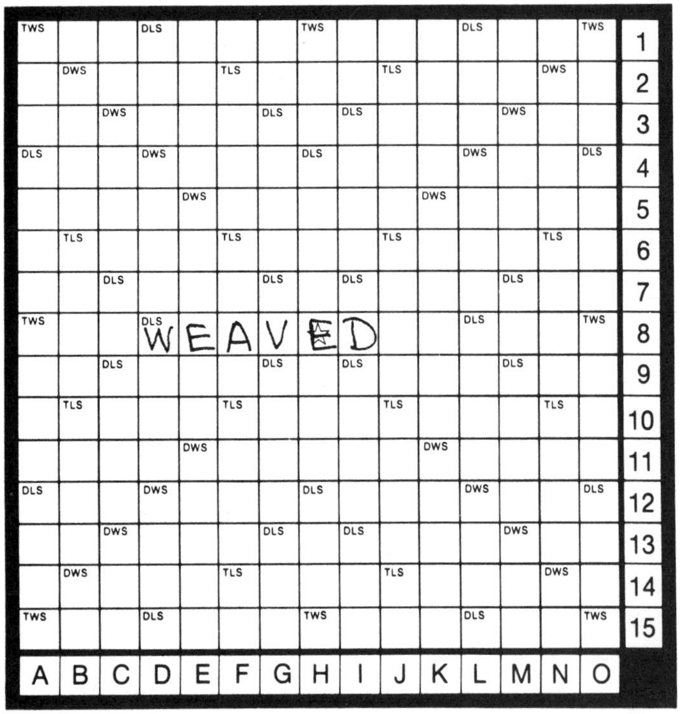

DIAGRAM 2

Rack	Play
QARRIED	Pass all 7 tiles

In Diagram 2, Player A has the tiles QARRIED. In this case, he would pass all seven tiles in hopes of drawing the high-valued tiles, or blanks, or S's which are still in the set.

An alternative play would be the word ARRIVED G 4-10. Although this plays away 6 tiles, the player must draw a U on his next turn to go with the Q in his rack. The odds against drawing a U make this play extremely risky. The 13 points the player gets for the word ARRIVED will not offset the loss of points over his next few turns should he keep the Q.

2. Middle Game Q-Strategy

In the middle stages of the game, a player should count the U's that are on the board to determine his course of action. Situation #1: Two or more U's have been played and Player A draws the Q. He has no U's or blanks so he should pass the Q. Situation #2: Player A has one of the few remaining U's but no Q. He should try to keep a U in his rack until the Q question is settled.

3. End Game Q-Strategy

In the later stages of the game, if the Q has not been played, there are several more courses of action. Situation #1: There are no spaces on the board for a Q. Player A draws the remaining U's in the set, but not the Q. He should try to keep the remaining U's. This would mean that his opponent might get stuck with the Q at the end of the game. Situation #2: There are no spaces on the board for the Q. Player A draws the remaining U's in the set, but not the Q.If he wants to play a U, he should make sure his opponent cannot play the Q on it.

D. The Blanks

The blanks are the most important tiles in the game. They are the equivalent of a wild card. When a player picks that wild card, he has a great advantage over the other players who have only cards of face value.

1. Play for a Bingo

The blank, itself, does not have any face value, as its point count is zero. Its great advantage lies in its potential of forming a Bingo—thus, an extra 50 points for the play. Whenever a player draws a blank, he should play a Bingo or develop his rack towards a Bingo and create a spot for it on the board.

If a player cannot put down a Bingo, he should keep the blank and play away letters that will leave his rack balanced. We do not, however, advocate the deliberate sacrifice of points; but a good intermediate play of 25 or 30 points should leave reasonable tiles in the rack to combine with a blank. Neither do we advocate fishing for a certain letter while a blank is in the rack. This would be bad strategy and would lead to a loss of time and points.

What we do advocate is keeping a balanced rack and developing it after each play. In this way, a Bingo will come naturally and, at the same time a player will score good intermediate points.

The blank is an offensive tool. It is far too valuable to be used defensively. Rather than using the blank to prevent an opponent from scoring, a player should use it to create a high-scoring play for himself that would counteract his opponent's play. The only exception to this is in the later stages of the game when there are no openings on the board for a Bingo.

2. The Q and the Blank

One of the few exceptions for using a blank other than for Bingo purposes, is when a player draws a Q and there are no remaining U's in the set. If a player is unable to pass the Q, he must use the blank to avoid being penalized for holding the Q at the end of the game.

3. No Bingo Possibilities

Sometimes (but not as often as you may think), a player with a blank cannot make a Bingo due to a rack full of high-valued tiles which don't combine well. In this particular instance, when a player can score 40 + points with high-valued tiles and a blank, he should do so. The reason is that he will not interrupt the flow of play and will not sacrifice needless points.

4. Two Blanks

On rare occasions, a player is fortunate enough to pick up two blanks. In Diagram 3 the game has just begun and Player A opens with DIRTY 8 H-L. Player B draws two blanks and the letters XHBTS. Although Player B has no vowels, he has a good Bingo, EXHIBITS I 5-12. This would be worth 75 points and is certainly a good play. However, it is not recommended in this particular instance.

The play BOX 7 G-I is worth 41 points and is advocated here since two blanks would not be wasted. By playing BOX, Player B would score 41 points and leave himself with a blank and the tiles HTS. With any kind of a good draw, Player B would have a Bingo on his next turn. If he is very unlucky, this gambit will not pay off; but it's a good risk and more often than not, proves profitable for a player. CAUTION: In order to try this gambit, a player must have high-point tiles to make the first play and a reasonable chance of using the second blank for a Bingo in the next turn or the following one. If not, it's wiser to use the two blanks in one Bingo.

DIAGRAM 3

Rack	Word	Play Notation	Score
□ □ XHBTS	B[O]X	7 G-I	41
	Rather than		
	[E]XHI̲B[I]TS	I 5-12	75

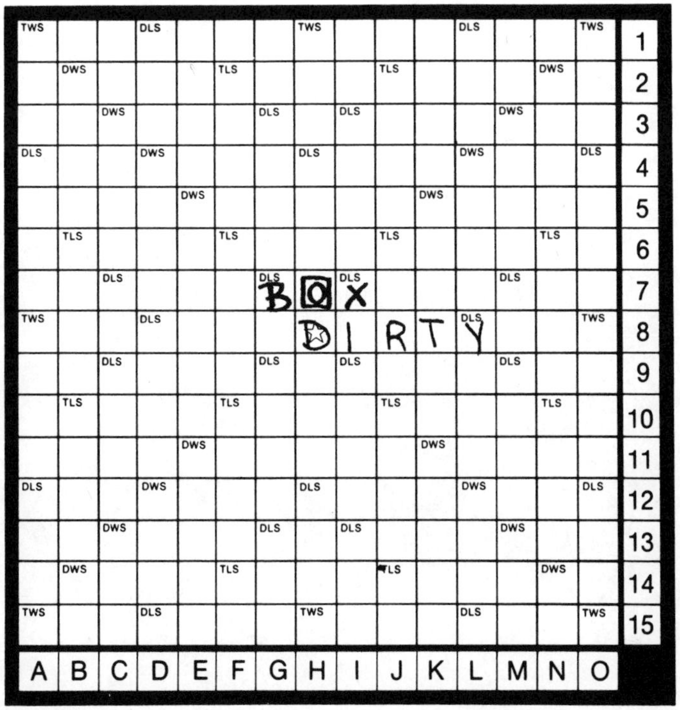

BOX
DIRTY
A B C D E F G H I J K L M N O
1 2 3 4 5 6 7 8 9 10 11 12 13 14 15

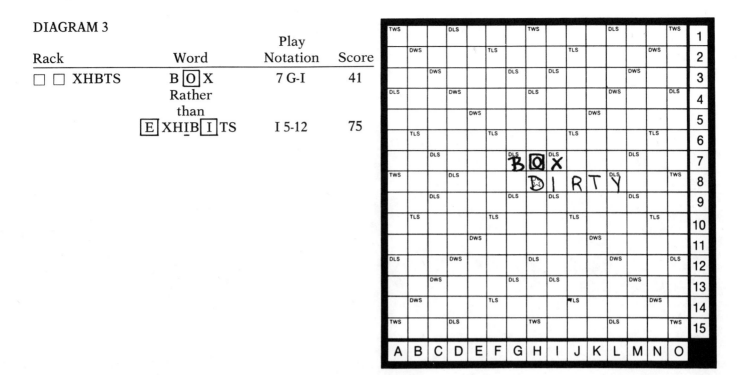

5. The Blank is Not a "Filler"

One final thought in the use of the two blanks. They should not be used merely as a filler for a poorly developed rack. If a player has no vowels or consonants (whichever the case may be), he should pass the tiles, keeping the blank, and attempt to draw new tiles to create a Bingo on his next play. In short, whenever a player has a blank, he should try to play a Bingo.

Having presented the importance of tile distribution and the letters, the discussion will now move on to the arbiter of SCRABBLE Crossword Game . . . the dictionary.

The Dictionary

Chapter 10

A. Getting To Know The Dictionary

There is one element that is not packaged in the SCRABBLE Crossword Game box—the knowledge of our language. As words are the vehicle for scoring, it is necessary to have a dictionary to determine which words are acceptable. This is the authority in deciding whether a play is legal or not.

Since every dictionary encompasses different parts of the English language, a good player must be familiar with the dictionary he uses—its quirks, limitations, and advantages. Although it is not necessary to know every word in the dictionary, there are some words a player must know in order to play well:

1) All the two-letter words (see Part 8).
2) A number of the frequently played three-letter words.
3) The words containing the high-valued letters of the game.

Such lists of words, added to a player's own vocabulary, make a smooth yet flexible game.

Since play proceeds by chaining words together, the links connecting the chains are, for the most part, two and three letter words. If a player has limited knowledge of these linking words, his play is definitely hampered.

Similarly, a good player should be familiar with words containing the high-valued letters: Q, X, J, Z. The more words containing these letters a player knows, the easier it will be for him to use these tiles to his advantage.

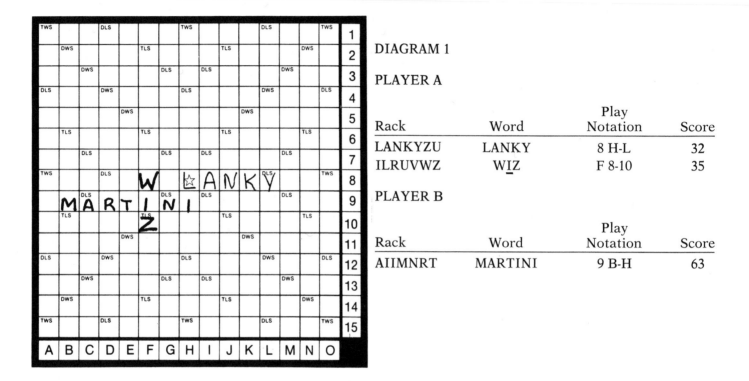

For example, in Diagram 1, Player A plays LANKY 8 H-L. Player B has a very nice Bingo, MARTINI, in his rack, but he must chain his Bingo to the word LANKY which is already on the board. If player B knows that LI is a word, he will be able to place his Bingo on the board for a 50 point bonus. Player A will then have to make a good play to compensate for his opponent's 50 point bonus. If player A knows his three letter words, he can play away the high-valued W and Z to form WIZ for 35 points.

1 2 3 4 5 6 7 8 9 10 11 12 13 14 15
A B C D E F G H I J K L M N O
LANKY
MARTINI
WIZ

DIAGRAM 1

PLAYER A

Rack	Word	Play Notation	Score
LANKYZU	LANKY	8 H-L	32
ILRUVWZ	WIZ	F 8-10	35

PLAYER B

Rack	Word	Play Notation	Score
AIIMNRT	MARTINI	9 B-H	63

SCRABBLE Crossword Game is not a game in which word meanings are a necessary requirement. However, it is necessary to know which part of speech a word is. This determines how the word is inflected. Can the word take the ending *er* or *est?* Can it be made plural? Can it take *ing* for a Bingo? If so, it is an offensive tool, as a player can add on letters.

Is the word a comparative form of an adjective or adverb? Is it a past tense of a verb? If so, it can be used in a defensive manner as the opponent cannot add anything to it. Knowing a word's part of speech aids a player in determining whether his opponent is bluffing or taking advantage of his creative vocabulary.

One of the most important parts of the dictionary is the sublist. These lists are comprised of prefixes and are a good source for Bingos. For instance, the prefix combinations *over, un,* and *re,* often come up in a player's rack. Becoming familiar with these lists enables a player to easily find his high-scoring Bingos.

This leads to the question: "Is the study of the dictionary necessary in order to play an expert game?" To a certain degree the answer is yes. Since word knowledge is the primary tool for all SCRABBLE Crossword Game players, the more words a player knows the better he will play. Of course, it is not necessary to memorize the entire dictionary—and a great majority of dictionary words never come up in a game; but it might be added that the dictionary is probably one of the most interesting books in the world to read.

B. Questions & Answers: Words

The following are questions that many players ask.

1. What Dictionary Should We Use?

Before the game begins, players should agree on the standard abridged dictionary they will use to settle all disputes during the game. Read the introduction to this dictionary so that all players will know how this particular dictionary deals with normal plurals, verb endings, etc.

2. What Words Are Acceptable?

All words listed in an abridged dictionary and labeled with a part of speech are acceptable, except: words always capitalized, abbreviations, prefixes and suffixes standing alone, and words requiring a hyphen, an apostrophe, or a period.

An acceptable word must be labeled with a part of speech: noun, verb, pronoun, adjective, adverb, preposition, conjunction, interjection.

This includes *all* words whether designated as of foreign origin or as archaic, obsolete, colloquial, slang, or given as an alternate spelling; however, any word used in the definition of a word but not listed in the dictionary, itself, will not be acceptable.

3. What About Words Designated as Foreign?

Many people have asked us what constitutes a foreign word, so we asked the editor of an abridged dictionary. He told us that all words found in an abridged source are used somewhere in our American/English language. Since only the most common foreign words that we use are in an abridged dictionary, they are acceptable as long as they follow the specifications set forth in Question #2.

4. Are Regular Plurals and Verb Endings Acceptable?

Read the introduction to your dictionary. You will find that most abridged dictionaries list plurals of nouns and verb endings in unusual situations only. Normal plurals of nouns and normal verb endings are acceptable. Unless otherwise specified, a noun can be made plural. Please note that interjections cannot be pluralized unless specifically stated in the dictionary.

5. What About Prefixes and Suffixes?

Prefixes and suffixes standing alone are not acceptable. To determine whether a word can take a prefix or not, the new word must be listed in either the main listing or the prefix sublisting. For example, the word *unable* is listed as an adjective in the main listing; therefore, it is acceptable. The word *unalike* is listed in the prefix "un" sublisting; therefore, it is acceptable. The word *unphoned* is not listed in either the main listing or the sublisting; therefore, it is *not* acceptable.

6. Are Chemical Symbols Acceptable?

No, they have no part of speech and are capitalized.

7. Why Are the Following Words Not Acceptable?

vs.: There's a period at the end: thus, an abbreviation and *not* acceptable.

OK (adv): Even though it has a part of speech, it is capitalized; thus, *not* acceptable.

wa' (n): Even though it has a part of speech, there is an apostrophe; thus, *not* acceptable.

non-: It has a hyphen, no part of speech, and is a prefix standing alone; thus, *not* acceptable.

zoot suit (n): Zoot cannot stand alone; thus, *not* acceptable.

8. What About Letters of the Alphabet?

As long as letters of the alphabet (this includes foreign alphabets) are in the main listing of the dictionary and are labeled with a part of speech, they are acceptable. Just as other nouns, they can be pluralized unless otherwise stated. Foreign letters listed under the word "Alphabet" are not acceptable unless they are listed separately in the dictionary. In club and tournament play, the letters of the English alphabet must be spelled out, i.e. *cee,* plural *cees,* as merely placing a *C* or *CS* on the board does not relate to the game.

9. Are Alternate Spellings Allowed?

Yes. For example:

1. xebec (n.) also spelled zebec. The word zebec is acceptable.
2. ax (n.). Also British, axe. The word axe is acceptable.
3. woeful (adj). Also Archaic woesome. The word woesome is acceptable.
4. zareba or zariba (n.). The word zariba is acceptable.

C. The SCRABBLE PLAYERS Dictionary

As players can tell by reading the preceding questions and answers, dictionary interpretation involves a great deal.

SCRABBLE PLAYERS has realized this problem and is presently working on the SCRABBLE PLAYERS Dictionary which will take the "guesswork" out of dictionary interpretation. It will contain *all* acceptable words of eight letters or less—all plurals, all verb endings, all comparative and superlative forms, all sublist words, all alternate spellings.

No longer will there be a question as to which words can take an S or ER or UN. All acceptable forms will be spelled out. As soon as the SCRABBLE PLAYERS Dictionary is completed, it will be the final authority in all SCRABBLE PLAYERS activities.

Closely linked with the study of the dictionary is the development of anagram skills. This next topic for discussion is essential for game improvement.

Anagrams

Chapter 11

The impetus to create SCRABBLE Crossword Game came from anagrams and crossword puzzles. Thus, any discussion of the game must include a chapter on anagrams, or how to form words from the letters in the rack.

In order to create words from random letters, a player should know basic word structures. These structures are most commonly found in the form of verb conjugations, comparative forms of adjectives and adverbs, prefixes and suffixes.

Perhaps the most common source of Bingos is the group of words ending with *ies, ing, ed, iest, er, est*. These letters are found in declensions of adverbs and adjectives, conjugations of verbs, and the plurals of certain nouns. The ending *ies* usually occurs as the plural of a noun ending in *Y*: baby—babies. The ending *ed* usually is added to any four or five letter verb in the language to form a Bingo.

The endings *er, est, ier,* and *iest,* are normally used as comparative or superlative forms of adjectives and adverbs. For instance: hard—harder—hardest; sandy—sandier—sandiest. These endings are also very useful in developing a balanced rack for a Bingo, since they contain those tiles most conducive for Bingo combinations.

Common suffixes to know are: *ate, ious, ous, tion, sion, tive, sive, cive, al, ial, ion, ian.* If a player sees these combinations in his rack, he should set them up at the end of his rack and look for remaining letters to form a Bingo.

The Latin and Greek words used as prefixes are also very handy to know. The most valuable are: *be, com, con, de, dis, ex, non, out, over, pro, pre, re, sub, un.* Other combining forms include: *ab, ad, ante, anti, bi, dia, hemi, in, inter, intra, neo, ob, para, per.* A good player will familiarize himself with these combining forms, as most of them have sublists in the dictionary.

In looking for prefixes and common endings, a player should not hesitate to use the tiles on the board as if they were in his own rack. Whenever an opponent opens up the board, a player should immediately look for these specific combinations to create a seven-letter Bingo, if not one of eight or nine letters.

Of course, our language is not created in a strict mold and many words cannot be broken down into specific structures. That is why a player must learn which letters of the alphabet combine to form common words. These combinations should then act as sign-posts so that automatically a player begins to look for words of a particular nature.

For words which don't have normal inflected forms, there are certain memory aids that many expert players have found helpful:

Outpain = Utopian
Horates = Earshot
Baronied = Debonair
Moraled = Earldom
Alomate = Oatmeal

When these tiles appear in a player's jumbled rack, it is mechanically easier for him to form normal word structures and allow his memory to work from there.

Just as important as knowing which letter combinations form Bingos, is knowing which letter combinations don't. This will help a player save time and energy by not looking for Bingos in letter combinations that do not contain any. Some common examples follow:

NAILERS
ADORNES
OARIEST
SKATIER

Anagram skill is not given to only a chosen few. Rather it is a knack that requires practice and concentration. Anyone who actively moves his tiles in his rack and uses the open tiles on the board, will quickly become good at finding anagrams in an assorted jumble of letters.

The greater number of words a player can find in a random bunch of letters, the greater his ability will be to choose between one play and another. This, in turn, will increase understanding of the strategic elements of the game.

This ends the section devoted to TACTICS—the "How to do it" elements of scoring, tile distribution, the letters of the alphabet, dictionary use, and anagram skill.

Now, it's time to move on to the "What to do" elements—the STRATEGY of SCRABBLE Crossword Game as analyzed through the different stages of the game . . . opening, middle, and end game.

Part 4

Strategy

This next section, devoted to STRATEGY, is divided into three parts: the Opening Game, the Middle Game, and the End Game.

Since there are many different techniques connected with each stage of the game, it is necessary to look very carefully at how to begin the game with good tiles; with poor tiles. What to do in the middle game when ahead; when behind. How to handle the last few moves to come out the winner.

All of this strategy is very important in order to become a good SCRABBLE Crossword Game player.

The Opening Game

Chapter 12

A. Beginning The Game With Good Tiles

1. Use the First Move to Give the Game Direction
The first move in almost all board games is considered to be an advantage. It's like having the first punch in a boxing match or being the first one to jump out of the starting gate in a race. In SCRABBLE Crossword Game, the first move gives a player a number of distinct advantages:

- It enables him to gain the lead. This, in itself, can mean as little as 10 points or as much as 110 points.
- It gives him the opportunity to develop his rack in accordance with the principles discussed in the chapter on tile development.
- It gives him the option of directing the game into any style he wishes.

Diagram 1 illustrates the last point. Player A has the option of playing one of two words—CAROB or COBRA. Both are anagrams of the letters ABCOR. Both words would be played in the same position (8 D-H) and score 24 points. Seemingly, there is very little difference between the two plays and it would be of minor significance to choose one above the other.

In this case, the play is dictated by the two tiles which are left in the rack. A player should select the play which leaves the best options for the tiles remaining in his rack. If his leave (the tiles remaining in his rack) consists of high-valued tiles, a player should try to close the board to Bingo possibilities and concentrate on the premium squares. If, however, a player's leave is conducive to Bingo possibilities, he should then play a word which opens up Bingo possibilities.

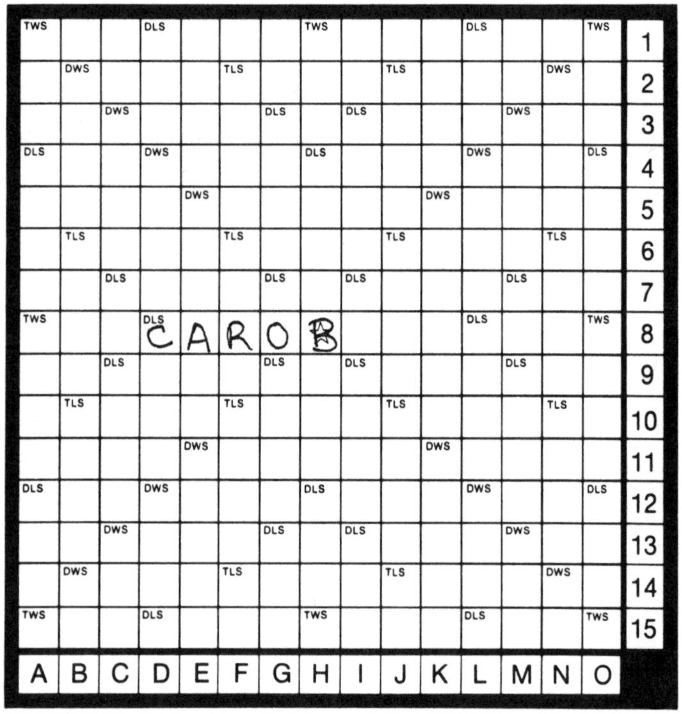
CAROB

DIAGRAM 1

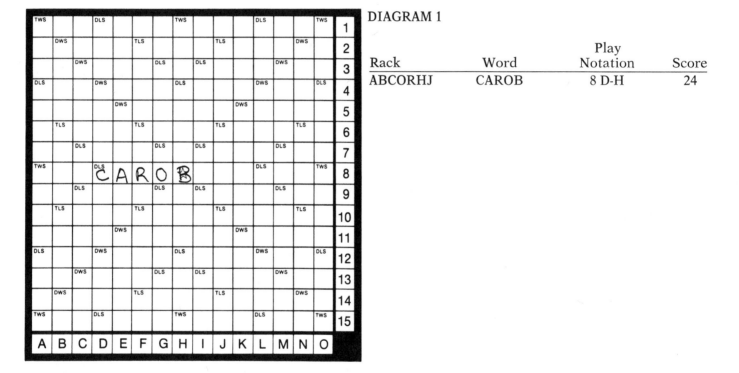

Rack	Word	Play Notation	Score
ABCORHJ	CAROB	8 D-H	24

a. High-valued leave

With the leave HJ, a player should play CAROB which opens the board to high-valued tiles and closes it to Bingo possibilities. Any high-valued tile could be placed on the double letter squares either above or below the O (G-8) for a good point count.

As we discussed previously, most Bingos are chained to the board by means of a two-letter word. The B ending in CAROB makes it difficult for an opponent to play a Bingo, as there are no two-letter words ending in B and only a few beginning with it.

DIAGRAM 2

Rack	Word	Play Notation	Score
ABCORES	COBRA	8 D-H	24

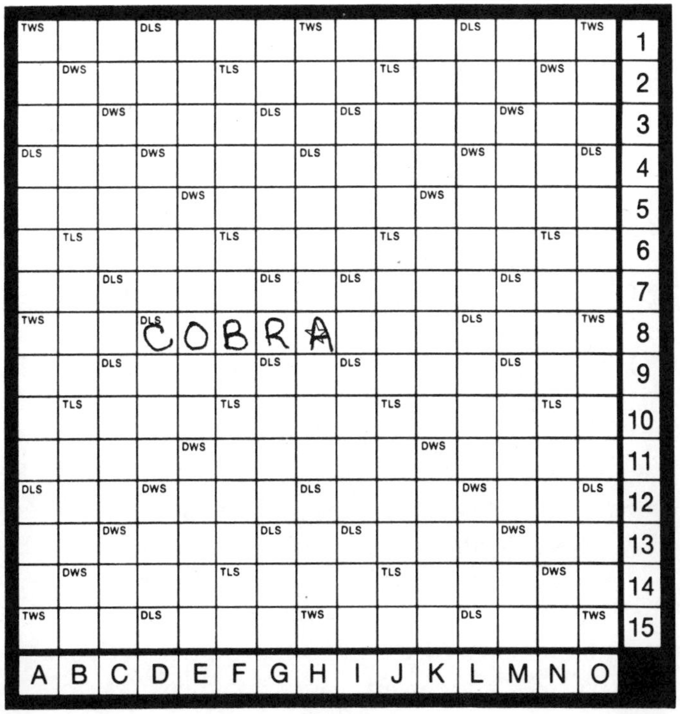

COBRA

b. Bingo prone leave

If, instead of having high-valued tiles, a player has the leave ES, he should play COBRA which opens the board to Bingo possibilities. The R on square 8-G blocks the double letter squares above and below it so that an opponent cannot place high-valued tiles there. To get a good score, the opponent is forced to open the board. The A ending in COBRA, which is placed on the middle square 8-H, is very conducive to Bingos, as almost any letter combination can be placed above or below it.

With the leave ES and an opponent who has opened the board, a player has many possibilities to play a Bingo within his next few turns.

2. Play for the First Bingo

In the opening stages of the game, a player should always play for the first Bingo. He should try to develop his Bingo tiles as quickly as possible because:

a) The board is relatively empty. It is much more difficult to play a Bingo in the later stages of the game when the board closes up.
b) The first Bingo allows a player to use more tiles and, thus, see more of the set's contents than his opponent.
c) The first Bingo puts a player in the immediate point lead—a substantial lead. This makes his opponent take chances in order to catch up.

What happens if the starting player has "an almost Bingo"? If Player A has the first move and draws the tiles SATIREK, he could place the S on the center square and play STRIKE 8 H-M for 30 points. Or he could pass the K in hopes of picking up one of the 18 tiles that combine with SATIRE to form a Bingo. His odds of drawing a Bingo tile are very good.

This is known as a gambit for position and advantage. It doesn't always work so there has to be a good chance of success in order to justify using it. If this gambit does not succeed, a player should not continue looking for a Bingo to the detriment of his score and position on the board. It would be silly for a player to throw away three or four turns, while his opponent is scoring high point plays.

3. Play Your Tiles in Quantity

During the early stages of the game, it is very important for a player to play away as many tiles as possible. Based on the 100 tiles in each set, a player, in turn, sees 7% of the set's contents. Since most of the valuable tiles are extremely likely to still be in the box, a player who plays 35 tiles to his opponent's 20, uses 15% more of the set's contents—or, at the very least, keeps his opponent from using them.

4. Strive for Rack Development

In the opening stages of the game, a player with good tiles usually has an option of playing any one of several plays that are equally good in point count. As the board is very open in these early stages, and there isn't much room for defense, a player should select the play that not only plays away tiles but also leaves him with good Bingo conducive tiles.

5. Attack is the Best Defense

The character of any particular game is not clearly defined until the fifth or sixth move. As has already been discussed, it is better to play offensively at this stage, than defensively since the board is quite open. A player with good tiles should be ready to "slug" it out with his opponent and try to outscore him. This, of course, should be done without ruining a player's rack or foolishly opening up good spots for his opponent.

6. Create Numerous Openings

When a player has good tiles, he is superior in force to his opponent. In the early stages of the game, a player should open lines and create numerous spots for his own scoring benefit. Even though this creates spots for his opponent, it also creates many possibilities for a player's own high scoring tiles. This is known as the principle of *"one for one,"* or *"two for one."*

For example, in Diagram 3 there are many spots open on the board. Player A has the tiles PYMVONE, which are not particularly conducive to Bingos but which are relatively balanced with vowels and high-valued intermediate consonants.

Player A must now decide which is the best move to make that will give him not only a good point count, but also leave good tiles in his rack. Player A could play VENOM 13 C-G, for 26 points, or ENVOY L 4-8 for 30 points. The only trouble with these two plays is that they don't guarantee Player A a good play on his next turn. Rather, they tend to close the board and not create spots for his remaining intermediate tiles.

DIAGRAM 3

PLAYER A

Rack	Word	Play Notation	Score
PYMVONE	VENOM	13 C-G	26
	ENVOY	L 4-8	30
	VENOM	E 1-5	28

VENOM
IRON
RATION
ENVOY
WINTER
WEATHER
VENOM
A B C D E F G H I J K L M N O
1 2 3 4 5 6 7 8 9 10 11 12 13 14 15

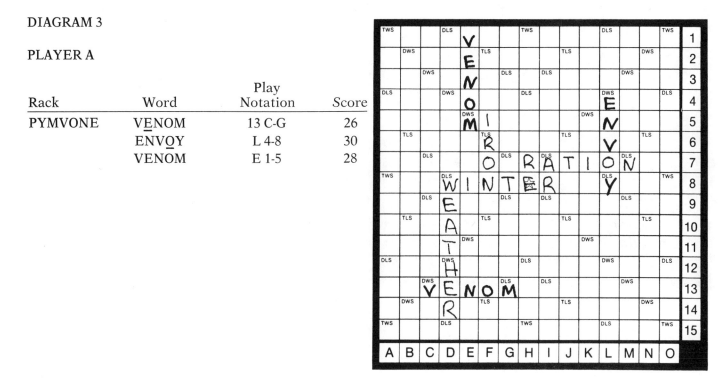

A preferable play would be VENOM, E 1-5. Although this play opens up the triple word square, 1-A, there are numerous high scoring spots on the board, such as 15-A and 8-O. There are also many spots for intermediate letters anywhere along the vowels on the board. Although this play may open a spot for Player B, it will also guarantee Player A a high scoring play for his next few turns.

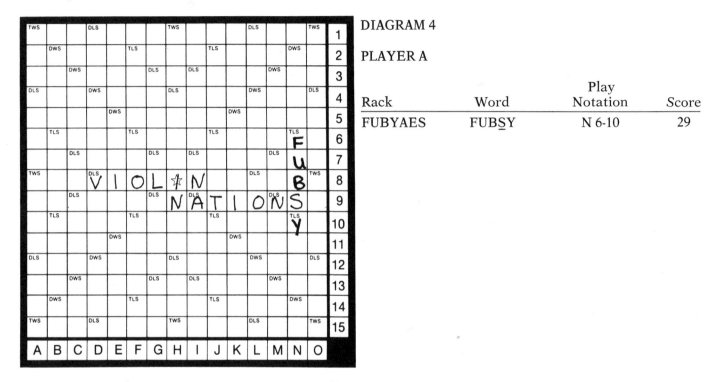

In Diagram 4, Player A has the tiles FUBYAES. If he plays FUBSY, N 6-10, for 29 points, he opens up the board for a number of high-point plays. His excellent leave is A, E, S. The F and Y already on the board can take an A in front of them; the B on the board, can take either A, E, or S after it for a triple word score. It is true that Player B could also take advantage of a particular spot, but Player A's excellent rack leave should place him in the lead.

VIOL★N
NATIONS
FUBSY

DIAGRAM 4

PLAYER A

Rack	Word	Play Notation	*Score*
FUBYAES	FUBSY	N 6-10	29

7. Use the Premium Squares

If a player does not have Bingo-prone tiles, he should place his intermediate tiles on a double or triple letter square for a good point count.

8. Hoard S's

The S's are the most important tiles in the opening stages of a game. When a player draws an S at this stage, he should keep it unless he has a very high scoring play. The player can then capitalize on all opening spots that his opponent is foolish enough to create. If, however, a player draws two S's, he should play one away for a good point count. Whether he plays an S or not, a player should keep track of how many S's are on the board.

9. Keep Track of the U's

As discussed in Chapter 9, a player should keep track of the U's until the Q question is settled.

B. Beginning The Game With Poor Tiles

Many players have had the misfortune of starting a game with poor tiles. Not knowing how to cope with this, they have begun losing the game with their first few turns. Fortunately, there are a number of good techniques which can remedy this seemingly hopeless situation.

1. Pass to Achieve Tile Flexibility

The merits of passing have been discussed in previous sections, but this is the first section that encourages passing for reasons other than playing for a Bingo. For instance, Player A starts the game with the rack AAILORN. He could play the five-letter word ALOIN for 12 points, or he could pass all seven tiles and start the game with seven new tiles. If Player A plays ALOIN, he gives his opponent the opportunity to play through several good vowels and consonants for a high-point play. Not only does Player B score more points, but Player A has done nothing to develop his rack. The recommended play is to pass all seven tiles and pick up seven new ones. The 12 points that Player A loses will more than likely be offset by the tiles he picks from the remainder of the set.

Don't forget, that Player A has already seen 7% of the set—by passing all seven of his tiles he will see 7% more. This gives him a very high probability of picking up seven good tiles—either high-valued or Bingo prone. Once again, notice that Player A passes all seven tiles regardless of vowels or consonants. He would, of course, keep all S's or blanks, as they are too valuable to pass.

Passing in the early stages of a game is less harmful than passing in the later stages, as the game has not yet taken on a particular pattern. Nor, has an opponent had a real opportunity to gain a commanding lead. A player is merely relinquishing his initiative to his opponent, but this does not necessarily mean that it will be a strong initiative or a decisive one.

2. Discourage High-Point Scoring Contests

If Player A has poor tiles in the beginning of the game, he should not encourage a scoring contest. After all, he cannot possibly outscore his opponent if his opponent has good tiles. This could lead to an irreparable loss of points for Player A. Of course, Player B with his good tiles, will want to encourage a high-point slugfest. Therefore, a variety of defensive techniques is advisable.

a. Avoid needless openings

A player should not open the lines of the board until he has tiles good enough to occupy them. The simplest way of doing this is by placing a word parallel to a word on the board as illustrated by the arrow in Diagram 5, 7 F-I. This interlocks a player's tiles with those already on the board and keeps the board closed. It is also advisable to use defensive words such as past tenses, plurals, and comparatives of adjectives and adverbs.

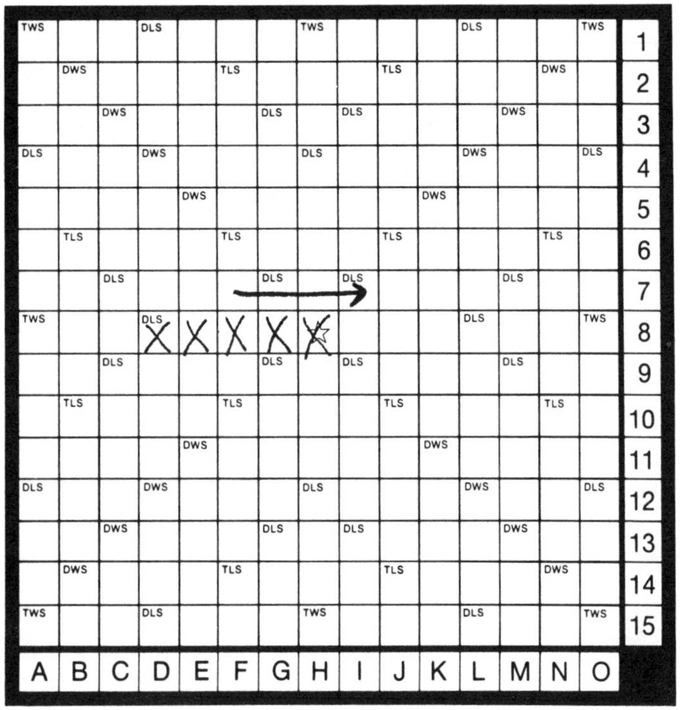

DIAGRAM 5

b. Block premium squares

Player B with his good tiles will concentrate on opening up the premium squares on the board. If he opens these spots, Player A should try to close them, or at least, place his tiles on them. This will prevent Player B from using these spots and will give Player A extra scoring for his relatively poor tiles.

c. Play in the most important spots first

When the board is so open that there are numerous spots to play in, a player with poor tiles should select the spot that would do the most harm to his opponent. For example, in Diagram 6, Player A has the rack GFLIOAL and is faced with several problems:

1) The board is wide open.
2) There are many vowels and consonants which his opponent can play through.

3) Player A has no substantial point scoring plays of his own.
4) His rack contains duplication of L.
5) He has vowels and consonants that don't combine well.

With all these problems, Player A would be very wise to play FILIAL, G 7-12 for 14 points. In this way, Player A gets rid of five tiles, including his duplication. Best of all, his F is on the only premium square, G-7, that is directly preceding a vowel. This spot would have undoubtedly been his opponent's choice. Notice, too, that the play FILIAL blocks the letters of the word ANOTHER E 8-14, so that it is more difficult for his opponent to play through these letters for any substantial scoring play. Player A has thus used his poor tiles to close the premium squares in addition to the line of play that would have been best for his opponent's better tiles.

DIAGRAM 6

PLAYER A

Rack	Word	Play Notation	Score
GFLIOAL	FILIAL	G 7-12	14

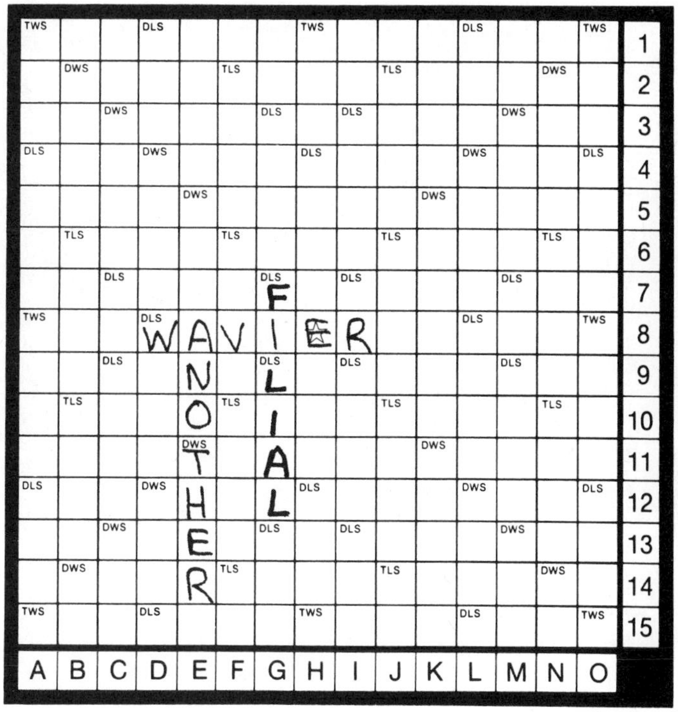

WAVIER
ANOTHER
FILIAL
A B C D E F G H I J K L M N O
1 2 3 4 5 6 7 8 9 10 11 12 13 14 15

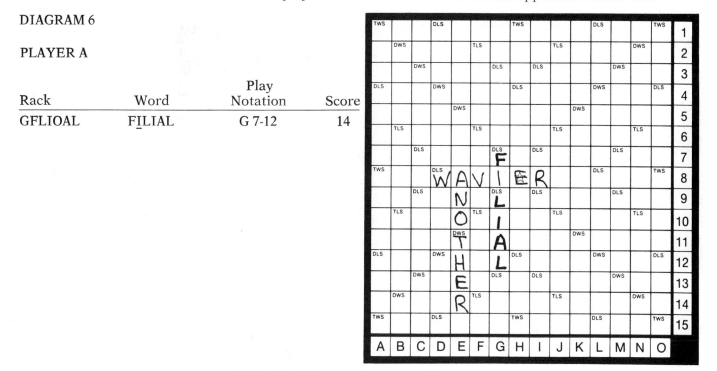

3. Do Not Make any Desperate Plays

If Player B gets an early lead with his good tiles, it would be wrong for Player A to make a risky play in order to try and catch up. Player A should develop his rack and wait until he has good tiles before he opens the board.

4. Play an Aggressive Defense

A player with poor tiles should have a definite direction in mind with each move he makes. His goal is not only to prevent his opponent from scoring, but also to develop his own rack and create spots for any good tiles he may hold. Even with poor tiles a player must be active rather than passive.

The Middle Game

Chapter 13

There are certain predominant patterns in the middle game which vary depending on whether a player is ahead or behind. In each case, it is very important for a player to pay special attention to tile management.

A. When Ahead

When a player is ahead in the middle game, he should try to maintain and/or increase his point lead. There are several ways of doing this.

1. Use the Intermediate High-Valued Tiles to Maintain the Lead

If a player plays words of 25 to 40 points on each of his turns, this places pressure on his opponent to try and keep up. The opponent is then forced to try to develop Bingo possibilities in his own rack which, in the long run, will probably result in loss of points during each of his turns.

2. Prevent S Spots on the Board

An S spot is any square on the board which can take an S such as a singular noun, a verb infinitive, etc. S Bingos are the easiest to play. By preventing S spots on the board, a player forces his opponent to look for more difficult Bingos. Common ways to close S spots on the board are:

a) the use of past tense verbs.
b) the use of comparative and superlative forms of adjectives and adverbs.
c) the use of words that take no letters before or after them.
d) the occasional use of an S to pluralize an open spot on the board, thus, preventing an opponent from using it.

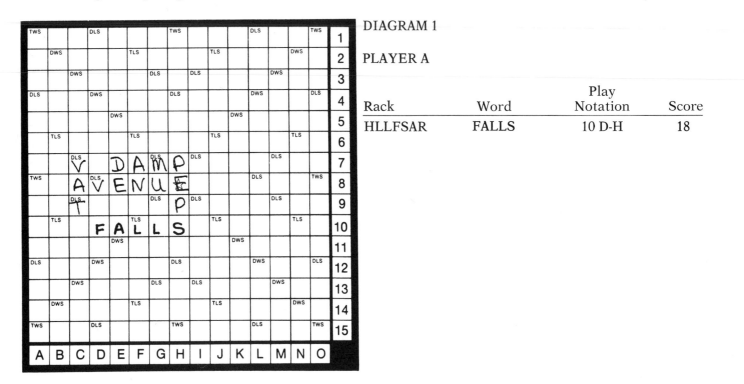

For example, in Diagram 1, Player A has the tiles HLLFSAR and plays FALLS 10 D-H for 18 points. The S blocks the board and keeps Player B from making an easy Bingo.

VDAMP
AVENUE
T
P
FALLS

DIAGRAM 1

PLAYER A

Rack	Word	Play Notation	Score
HLLFSAR	FALLS	10 D-H	18

3. Allow Opponent Room for Only 8 or 9 Letter Bingos
This makes it even harder for an opponent to place a Bonus word on the board as he would have to develop his rack to a greater degree. Such rack improvement means loss of time and point count which will offset the points for his Bingo, should he play one. If he doesn't, he will fall hopelessly behind.

4. Close the Board
Although it is not possible to completely block the board, a player should impede his opponent as much as possible. For example, in Diagram 2, the arrowed lines represent words ending in S. If Player A assumes that his opponent has good tiles and is playing for a Bingo, Player A has to block the board. The best block would be one of the words described in A. 2 of this chapter (past tense, etc.) played along the line H 6-11.

DIAGRAM 2

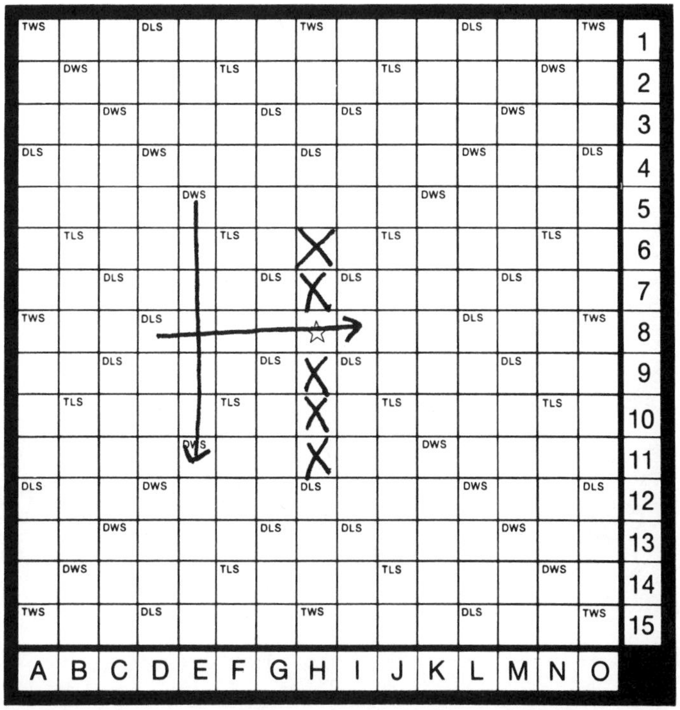
A B C D E F G H I J K L M N O
1 2 3 4 5 6 7 8 9 10 11 12 13 14 15

Diagram 3 shows a position that cannot be blocked completely. With the play 9 G-J, however, Player A can force his opponent to play his Bingo immediately (and most likely only in the area of the wavy line K 1-8). If Player B doesn't play his Bingo, Player A will be in a position to completely block the spot from any easy Bingo play.

DIAGRAM 3

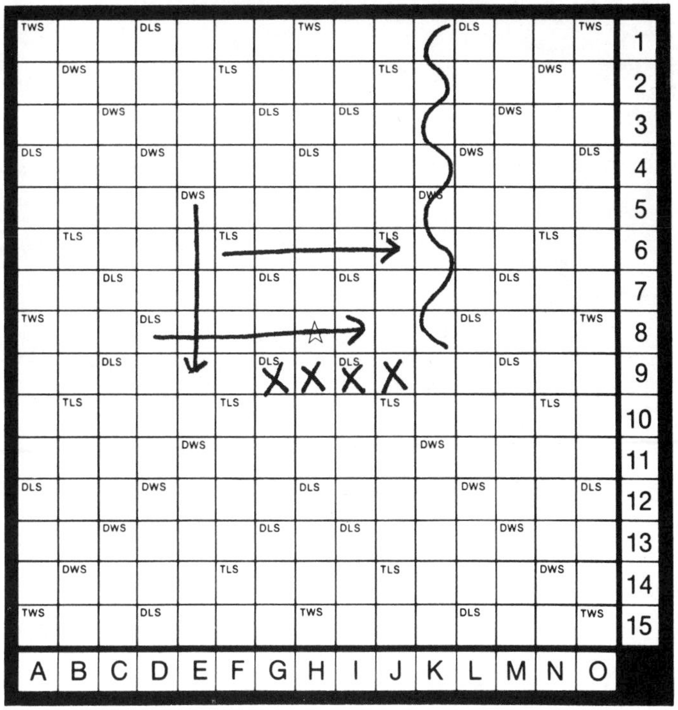
A B C D E F G H I J K L M N O
1 2 3 4 5 6 7 8 9 10 11 12 13 14 15

B. When Behind

When an opponent has played the first Bingo, or has taken an early lead, it is necessary for the player who is behind to make certain moves which are aggressive in nature but not foolhardy.

1) He *should not* take the highest point count play if it opens a correspondingly high or higher scoring spot for his opponent.
2) He *should not* attempt to open the board until he has developed his rack.
3) He *should not* fish for a Bingo unless his expectations for a Bingo are at least 50%.
4) He *should* open at least two spots for his Bingo attempt on any one play.

C. Counting

In the middle game, a player should count the major tiles (X, J, Z, K, Q) thus determining whether it is safe to leave premium squares unblocked. Then he should count S's and blanks to determine the danger of a Bingo from his opponent or the possibility of a Bingo for himself. Often those important letters are played away quickly. A good player keeps count of such plays and uses them to his advantage.

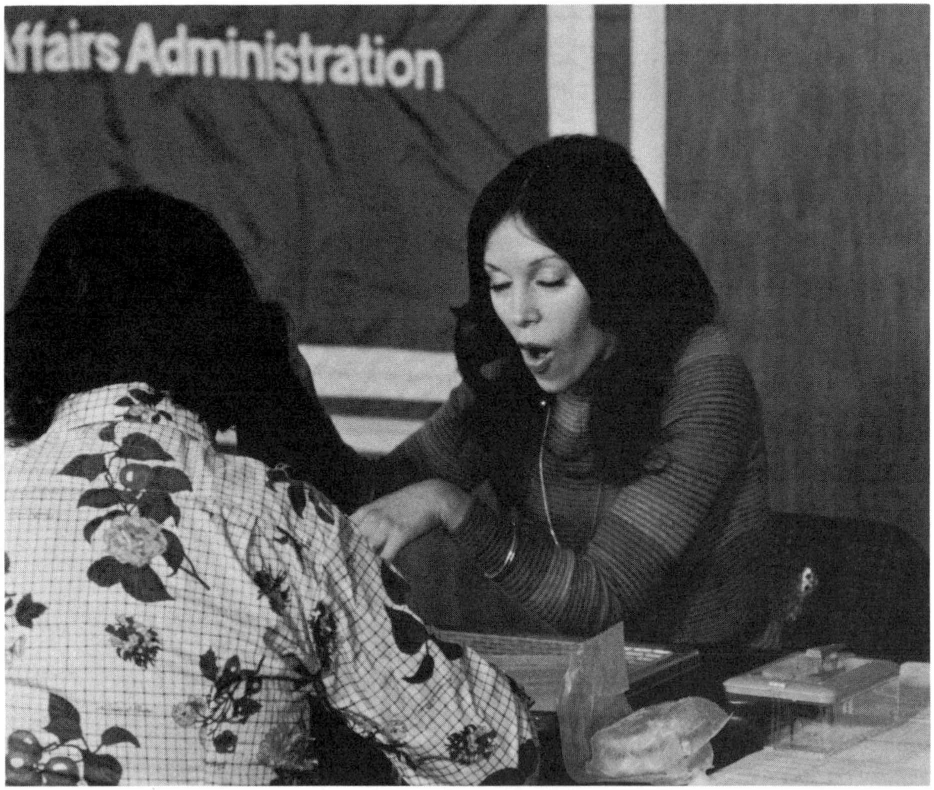
ffairs Administration

Chapter 14

The End Game

The end game strategy is very important. Its objectives are three-fold:

1) Use as many remaining openings as possible
2) Go out first
3) Try to catch your opponent with high-valued tiles.

A player should always try to go out first. With less than seven tiles (or no tiles at all) remaining in the set, a player should try to go out within two turns and catch his opponent with high-valued tiles. In order to do this, a good player counts tiles—particularly the important ones:

Z, X, J, Q, K
Four S's
Four U's
Two blanks

If one or more major tiles are still in the set towards the end of the game, a player should do one of two things:

a) Reduce the number of tiles he plays to lessen the chances of picking the undesirable tile, or
b) Prepare his rack so that he would be able to play away the major tile should he draw it.

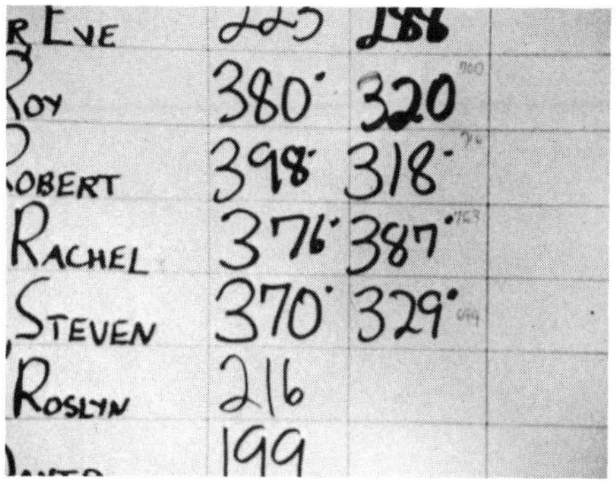
380 320
398 318
RACHEL 376 387
STEVEN 370 329
ROSLYN 216
199

According to the Club and Tournament rules, a player may pass at any point in the game provided there is a minimum of seven tiles remaining in the set (see Chapter 4). If there are less than seven tiles, and there is enough time remaining on the clock, a player should try to determine what his opponent is holding. If Player B is holding one of the major tiles, Player A should count the remaining vowels to see what plays are available to his opponent. Then, if possible, Player A should try to block Player B's use of the vowels.

If Player A has successfully blocked Player B, Player A may then proceed to play away one tile at a time for maximum point count (time permitting). For instance, in Diagram 1, assuming that the board is closed except for the word DING, 1 E-H and Player B is stuck with the Q with no place to play it. Player A has the tiles SPEN. Instead of playing SPENDING 1 A-H, for 39 points, Player A should get the maximum point count by playing:

ENDING, 1 C-H, for	9 pts.
PENDING, 1B-H, for	11 pts.
SPENDING, 1 A-H, for	36 pts.
Total	56 pts.

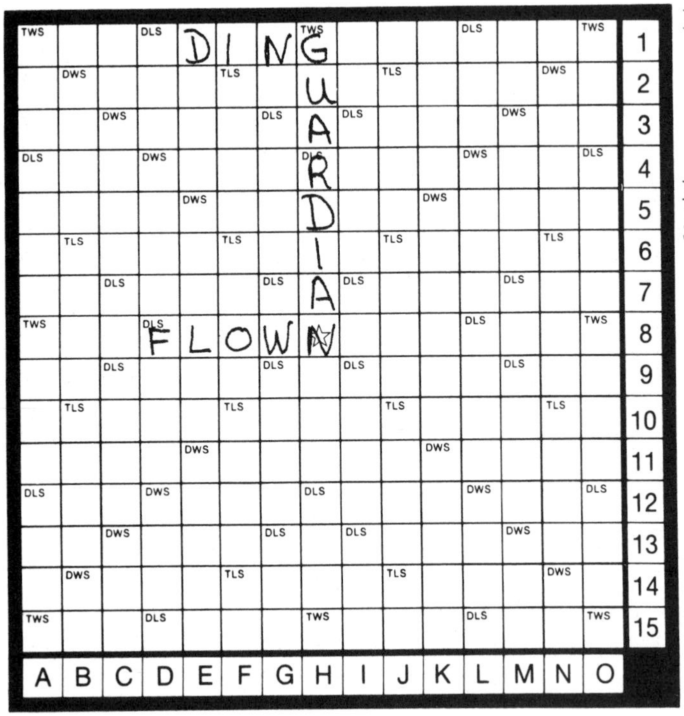

DING
GUARDIAN
FLOWN
A B C D E F G H I J K L M N O
1 2 3 4 5 6 7 8 9 10 11 12 13 14 15

DIAGRAM 1

PLAYER A

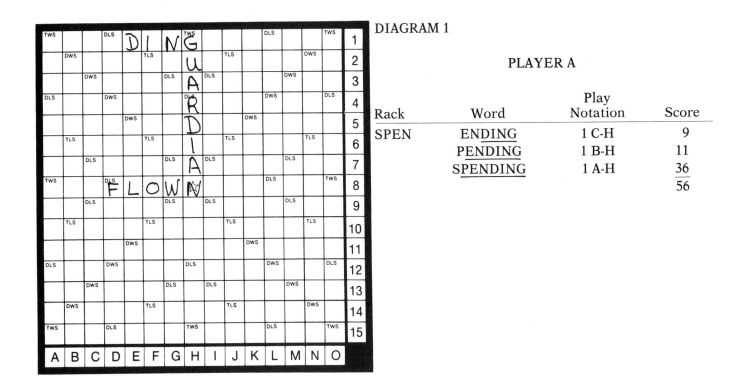

Rack	Word	Play Notation	Score
SPEN	ENDING	1 C-H	9
	PENDING	1 B-H	11
	SPENDING	1 A-H	36
			56

Now that tactics and strategy have been thoroughly discussed, it is time to move on to Part 5 of this Handbook, an addendum to both tactics and strategy.

This addendum includes the importance of tile counting; suggestions regarding the time to bluff and the time to challenge; and a summary of various styles of game play.

Part 5

Addendum To Tactics And Strategy

Chapter 15

Tile Counting

Counting tiles can make the difference between a winner and a loser. Many players never bother to count tiles and thus have no idea what their opponents have in their racks. If a player counts tiles, he has a good idea of what his opponent is holding.

Counting tiles is very important throughout all stages of a game—particularly in the advanced middle game and end game stages.

Tile counting in the opening game consists mainly of U's and S's. In the middle game, a player should still count U's and S's but should also keep an eye on the high-valued tiles. In the end game, he should count all important tiles:

Z, J, Q, X, K
Four S's
Four U's
Two blanks

At this stage, it's often necessary to count vowels to block an opponent from playing his high-valued tiles, or to create spots for a player's own letters.

Although it is usually impossible to keep a totally accurate count of all letters played, a player has something else to fall back on . . . logical assumption.

If for example, an opponent plays a word with two A's in it, a player can assume that his opponent does not have a third A in his rack.

All of this is part of the fun and excitement of SCRABBLE Crossword Game. When an opponent puts the other player in a ticklish situation, the other's ability to respond makes up the mind-challenging aspects of the game.

Chapter 16

Bluffs And Challenges

Another very important aspect of SCRABBLE Crossword Game is the area of bluffs and challenges. At times, a player has to play a phony word. At other times he has to keep his opponent honest by challenging an occasional dubious play.

These techniques can be very useful to every player, but there are certain guidelines to follow.

A. When To Bluff

A player should place a phony word on the board when:

1. His opponent has been wrong in his previous challenges.

2. His opponent would fall far behind should he challenge and be wrong.

3. It is his only chance of winning the game. At this point, the phony word should look very plausible or so outlandish that an opponent wouldn't dare challenge it.

B. When To Challenge

A player should not challenge if:

1. An opponent puts down a word which opens up a higher scoring possibility for the player's own letters.

2. An opponent plays a high scoring word and there is another spot open on the board where he could have played the same letters for a similar score.

3. An opponent plays a Bingo whose letters are so good that it has to be legitimate.

4. An opponent plays a Bingo whose anagrams could form another Bingo.

These techniques can add a great deal of fun to any game. If a player is able to buffalo his opponent into accepting all his words—good or bad—that player will almost always be a winner.

WORD CHALLENGED
Ka
acceptable
not acceptable

Various Styles Of Play

Chapter 17

In most games, individual players have different styles of play; SCRABBLE Crossword Game players are no exception.

Often it is not enough to simply follow the suggestions in the Handbook regarding tile distribution, blocking, etc. Other elements such as experience, judgment, and style are equally important.

A player whose objective is merely to win a game differs from a player whose objective is to carry on a running battle and win by a decisive margin.

The conservative player will try to tightly control the direction of the game by keeping the board relatively closed, and safe from an opponent's unexpected comebacks.

The dynamic player, on the other hand, will try to open the board to encourage scoring, not to mention increase his opponent's tension. Usually in this type of play, one player scores a decisive victory over the other.

The third type of player is one who incorporates both styles of play into his game. He is able to adjust to almost any competitive situation. His game experience is broader and more enjoyable than that of a restricted player.

In any case, all three styles of play have proven successful, which is a testimony to the game's strengths. However, it should be noted that styles of play without strategic principles are worthless. Used together, they make a highly enjoyable and successful game.

Part 6

Game Section

This section is, in effect, a final product. Throughout the preceding chapters of this Handbook, basic tactics and strategy have been discussed. During the play of an actual game, however, a player is often faced with a number of strategic and tactical themes which demand attention at the same time. Thus, a player must recognize the various problems and decide which of them deserves priority.

The following six games are presented to show how two excellent players attempt to solve the various problems that face them during a game. Each game is carefully annotated to determine how successful each player was. While the games may not be perfectly played in every case, they are of top-notch quality.

Game 1

The following game illustrates how exciting a wide open game can be. Both players are trying to "outslug" the other. An oversight by Player A as early as the 2nd turn, can account for his loss.

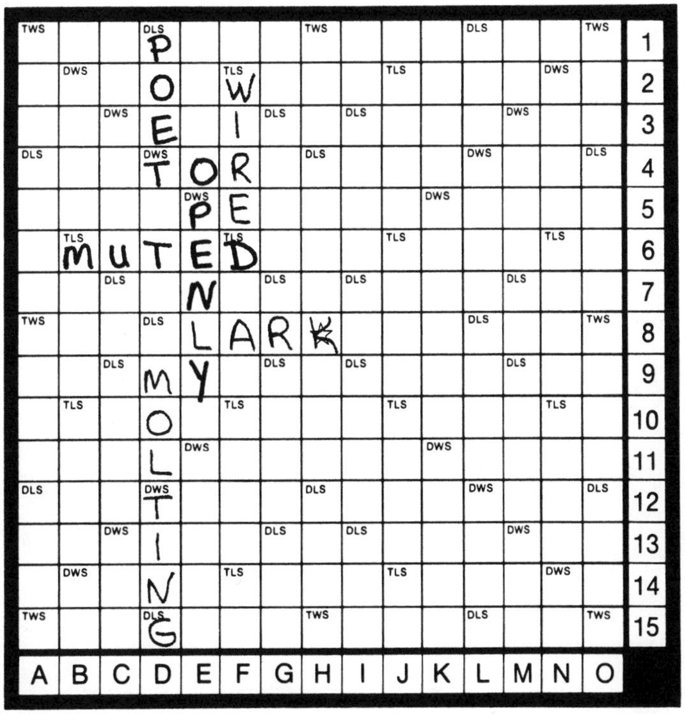

GAME 1
DIAGRAM 1
After B's 3rd turn

PLAYER A

	Rack	Word	Play Notation	Score
1.	AEIKLRR	LARK	8 E-H	16

LAKIER 8 G-L was preferable. It is 6 more points and 2 extra tiles played.

	Rack	Word	Play Notation	Score
2.	EIRINTW	WIRE	F 2-5	+21 / 37

An oversight. WINTRIER G 4-11 for 63 points was clearly best.

	Rack	Word	Play Notation	Score
3.	INTGMOL	MOLTING	D 9-15	+81 / 118

Clearly the only reasonable play.

PLAYER B

Rack	Word	Play Notation	Score
EMNOPPY	OPENLY	E 4-9	22

B tries to play as many tiles as possible.

Rack	Word	Play Notation	Score
MPDOTTU	MUTED	6 B-F	+31 / 53

A good play considering Player B's awkward tiles.

Rack	Word	Play Notation	Score
POTEQSU	POET	D 1-4	+24 / 77

This is a difficult play to decide upon. B reasons that since he could not profitably block the G along the triple word score (15-A), he would open up another triple word score. In this way he would be relatively sure of a large play with the Q next turn. A reasonable alternate was the play QUIP 13 B-E. This would have opened up another triple (EQUIP 13 A-E) and left B with excellent tiles.

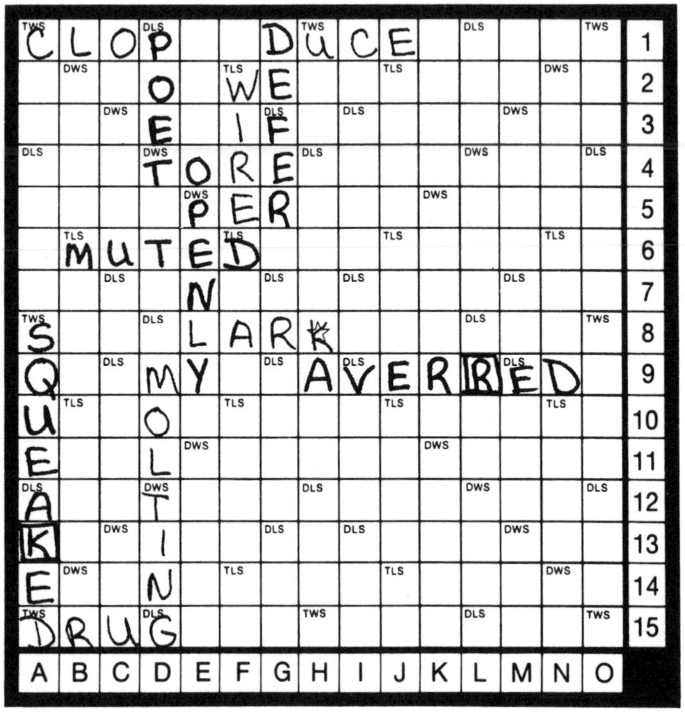

GAME 1
DIAGRAM 2
After B's 6th turn

PLAYER A

	Rack	Word	Play Notation	Score
4.	CDORUUX	DRUG	15 A-D	+18 / 136

A blocks a triple word spot and attempts to improve an awkward set of tiles.

	Rack	Word	Play Notation	Score
5.	COUXELS	CLOP	1 A-D	+24 / 160

A is still attempting to improve his rack. However, the play SILEX for 40 points (13 C-G) would have been better.

	Rack	Word	Play Notation	Score
6.	UXECGIS	DUCE	1 G-J	+21 / 181

A fills in the triple word spot and also sets up a play for his X on the square 2-J.

PLAYER B

Rack	Word	Play Notation	Score
QSUAEE□	SQUEA[K]ED	A 8-15	+104 / 181

An unexpected bonus. B has other Bingos, but this is the best.

Rack	Word	Play Notation	Score
ADEEEFR	DEFER	G 1-5	+36 / 217

This play is safer than first appears. It will actually be quite difficult for B's opponent to score substantially more than 36 points. Players with a conservative bent would prefer the play FREAKED H 4-10 for 19 points which is also perfectly acceptable.

Rack	Word	Play Notation	Score
AEDERV□	AVER[R]ED	9 H-N	+71 / 288

B picks a lucky rack and responds immediately with a second Bingo.

GAME 1
DIAGRAM 3
After B's 9th turn

	PLAYER A Rack	Word	Play Notation	Score	PLAYER B Rack	Word	Play Notation	Score
7.	XGISAGS	XI	2 J-K	+50 231	FIINOVZ	FIZ	3 K-M	+35 323
	Mandatory				The best play as it leaves the most flexible set of tiles.			
8.	GSAGSAS	GAS	10 F-H	+15 246	INOVHNN	OVINE	J 5-9	+16 339
	It seems that GAGES J 6-10 would be better, but perhaps it is only a matter of taste here.				B decided upon this play rather than attempt to rid himself of 2N's with the play NINE J 6-9. (Not NONE J 6-9 which would create an excellent spot on the I-7 square for the as yet unplayed J.)			
9.	GSASBNJ	BAN	8 M-O	+22 268	HNNOORY	YON	10 M-O	+22 361
	Somewhat risky as this play leaves Player A without a vowel. Since there are very few S spots on the board, the unusual play JOBS 5 I-L seems preferable.				HORNY 5 I-M was also good.			

A B C D E F G H I J K L M N O
1 2 3 4 5 6 7 8 9 10 11 12 13 14 15

GAME 1
DIAGRAM 4
FINAL POSITION

	PLAYER A Rack	Word	Play Notation	Score	PLAYER B Rack	Word	Play Notation	Score
10.	GSSJAEH	JAGS	11 J-M	+33 301	HNORIBE	NOH	12 I-K	+20 381
	As good a play as any.				B hopes to use his B on JO (J 11-13). Since he is substantially ahead, he tries to prevent Player A from playing a Bingo by closing the board.			
11.	SEHOLIT	NEOLITHS	14 D-K	+71 372	RIBEATI	IRATE	15 K-O	+20 401
	A brilliant play which nearly turns the game around.				Just enough to win.			
12.	AAITW	WIT	H 13-15	+18	BI	BIT	N 13-15	+10 411
	He could have gone out with ATWAIN O 3-8, but the final result would be the same.							
	Remaining tiles: A, A, I 3 points x 2 = 6			Total 390				+ 6 Total 417

Game 2

A game played brilliantly by both sides. B finally wins in the end-game when A gets caught with the Q.

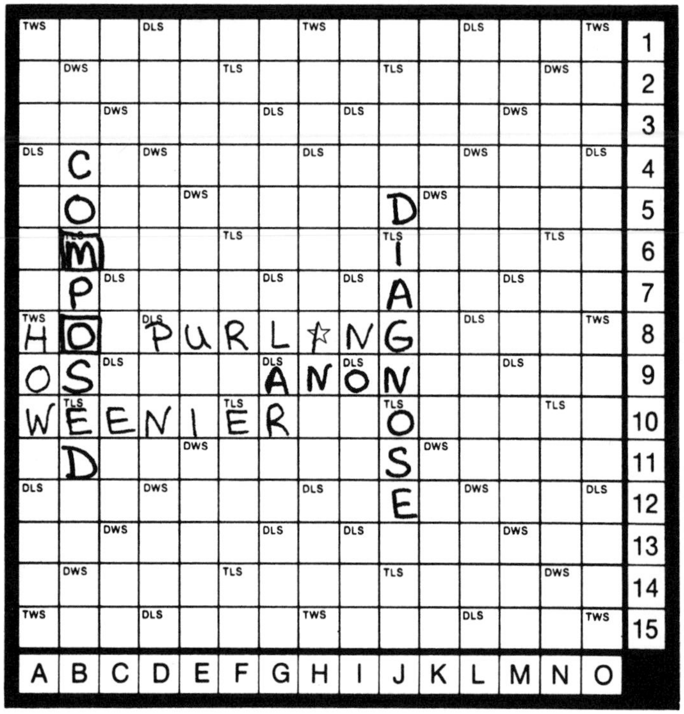

GAME 2
DIAGRAM 1
Position after B's 4th turn.

PLAYER A

	Rack	Word	Play Notation	Score
1.	ILNPRUW	PURLIN	8 D-I	22

The WU combination in A's rack handcuffs his chances for a big play, but he fortunately finds PURLIN.

	Rack	Word	Play Notation	Score
2.	WEEEINR	WEENIER	10 A-G	+67 / 89

A good Bingo.

	Rack	Word	Play Notation	Score
3.	ADIITTT	Pass all 7		+ 0 / 89

A can play TAW A 8-10 for 23 points, but this would leave his rack hopelessly imbalanced. He passes while the game is still young.

	Rack	Word	Play Notation	Score
4.	ABHIOUS	HOW	A 8-10	+41 / 130

The alternative was HAW in the same spot.

PLAYER B

Rack	Word	Play Notation	Score
ANNOOPS	ANON	9 G-J	14

B plays ANON to rid his rack of duplication.

Rack	Word	Play Notation	Score
OPSCD□□	CO[M]P[O]SED	B 4-11	+61 / 75

A very lucky draw. The unusually awkward board, however, allows B only this Bingo.

Rack	Word	Play Notation	Score
ENNUUTV	Pass all 7		+ 0 / 75

B is in the same predicament as A. Note that both players pass all their tiles.

Rack	Word	Play Notation	Score
ADGEIOS	DIAGNOSE	J 5-12	+74 / 149

A brilliant Bingo.

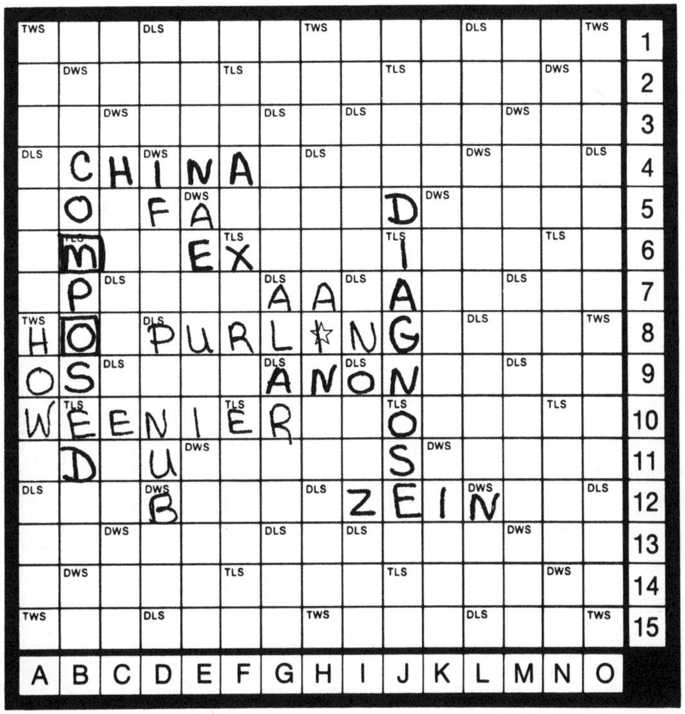

A B C D E F G H I J K L M N O

GAME 2
DIAGRAM 2
Position after B's 7th turn.

	PLAYER A				PLAYER B			
	Rack	Word	Play Notation	Score	Rack	Word	Play Notation	Score
5.	ABIUSAA	AA	7 G-H	+11 / 141	AEHIINT	CHINA	4 B-F	+20 / 169
	An unlucky draw forces A to try to rebalance his rack.				Keeping a balanced rack leave.			
6.	ABIUSEF	FA	5 D-E	+19 / 160	EITNVXZ	ZEIN	12 I-L	+26 / 195
	A still maneuvers for an improved rack.				Since the X is easier to play away for good points, B safely plays his Z in a spot that is comparatively safe from his opponent. Note that B keeps his E—a must as he is going to keep the X.			
7.	BIUSEAT	NUB	D 10-12	+10 / 170	ETVXETU	EX	6 E-F	+28 / 223
	With such good tiles, A starts "fishing" for a Bingo.				B knows A is fishing but decides to take points rather than defend. His policy appears to be correct, as it would be impossible to block the board significantly.			

GAME 2
DIAGRAM 3
Position after B's 11th turn.

PLAYER A

	Rack	Word	Play Notation	Score
8.	ISEATEI	IDEA	5 I-L	+10 / 180

Having picked poorly, A still plays to keep his rack balanced.

	Rack	Word	Play Notation	Score
9.	STEIALW	FLAW	1 L-O	+30 / 210

Not having a Bingo, A occupies the triple word square and keeps a balanced leave.

	Rack	Word	Play Notation	Score
10.	STEIBES	BESET	M 10-14	+28 / 238

An excellent play. Still not having a Bingo, A gets 28 points and creates a spot for the last S along the triple word score.

	Rack	Word	Play Notation	Score
11.	SIDEMOR	MISDOER	13 B-H	+78 / 316

A fine play.

PLAYER B

Rack	Word	Play Notation	Score
ETVTUFO	FOVEA	L 1-5	+30 / 253

Being well ahead, B plays boldly to increase his lead. Note he keeps his U as the game has reached its latter portion and the Q has not appeared.

Rack	Word	Play Notation	Score
TTUGLOT	TOOT	2 K-N	+14 / 267

This play both blocks the board and balances his rack.

Rack	Word	Play Notation	Score
TUGLAEO	GLOAT	14 I-M	+ 8 / 275

B feels compelled to partially block the dangerous spot A opened with his last play.

Rack	Word	Play Notation	Score
TUEGMVY	GYM	N 9-11	+36 / 311

Having lost his lead, B makes a bold but risky play to recover the lead.

GAME 2
DIAGRAM 4
FINAL POSITION

	PLAYER A Rack	Word	Play Notation	Score	PLAYER B Rack	Word	Play Notation	Score
12.	DJKLRTY	JOY	F 12-14	+21 337	TUEVEIT	EVITE	O 11-15	+41 352
	Having no vowels, A does the best he can.				A good play which gives B the lead. But where is the Q?			
13.	DKLRTRQ	KIT	I 4-6	+ 9 346	TUCIRU	CUT	14 A-C	+20 372
	A now knows he has no chance to win as B has the last two U's along with CIRT. He sees no way to trap B with one of his tiles, so he tries to make the best of a bad bargain.				B can take his time, as A is helpless.			
14.	DLRRQ	FOVEAL	L 1-6	+12 358	IRU	UP	D 7-8	+ 4 376
15.	DRRQ	DOR	10 I-K	+ 8 366	IR	RE	4 K-L	+ 4 380
16.	RQ	AR	L 14-15	+ 3	I	PIU	7 B-D	+ 6 386
	Remaining tile: Q 10 points x 2 = 20							+ 20
				Total 369				Total 406

Game 3

This game starts out well but then bogs down when A refuses to pass his Q. When he finally does pass, it's too late.

GAME 3
DIAGRAM 1
Position after B's 5th turn.

	PLAYER A Rack	Word	Play Notation	Score	PLAYER B Rack	Word	Play Notation	Score
1.	AAEEORT	AERATE	8 E-J	12	PHILIDS	HIP	7 H-J	21
	A clears his rack for six new tiles.				Not very imaginative, but it's worth 21 points.			
2.	OAIILRF	FILARIA	E 5-11	+40 52	LIDSVIX	LIVID	D 11-15	+24 45
	A has the beautiful Bingo AIRFOIL but unfortunately no place to play it. He compensates nicely, however, with this double-double score.				A bold play. He could have played SIX D 4-6 for 34 points, but he did not wish to use his important S. B is prepared to slug it out with his opponent.			
3.	OYAONEU	YAUD	15 A-D	+24 76	SXPNGEN	PIX	6 D-F	+28 73
	A poor rack. A does the best he can.				B is not happy with his rack, but he can at least play his X for a good score.			
4.	ONEOEED	Pass 7		+ 0 76	SNGENES	GENS	K 4-7	+19 92
	DOPE D 4-7 was the alternative, but A wants better tiles now.				B balances his rack.			
5.	MQARTOE	MOVER	13 B-F	+20 96	SNEO□RG	IGNORE[R]S	10 E-L	+64 156
	A is disappointed. The Q minus the U handcuffs his rack. Still, he must make a play...				B is quite satisfied with his rack and responds with a Bingo.			

A B C D E F G H I J K L M N O
1 2 3 4 5 6 7 8 9 10 11 12 13 14 15

GAME 3
DIAGRAM 2
Position after B's 10th turn.

PLAYER A

	Rack	Word	Play Notation	Score	Comment
6.	QATEIFO	FOGIE	4 I-M	+18 / 114	A really can do nothing until he draws a U. But he is unwilling to pass.
7.	QATMWOT	WONT	6 I-L	+22 / 136	Still looking for a U.
8.	QATMDKA	Pass 7		+ 0 / 136	All that waiting is for nothing
9.	AELTS□D	[B] LASTED	N 1-7	+78 / 214	A was richly rewarded for finally making the correct play.
10.	QURMHZB	BAH	3 M-O	+24 / 238	A's tiles look clumsy but will play well on this closed board. At least this time he got the Q with a U.

PLAYER B

	Rack	Word	Play Notation	Score	Comment
6.	DOEYOUI	OUI	3 G-I	+11 / 167	Not so much for defense as to balance his rack.
7.	DOEYBTA	BOOTY	G 2-6	+26 / 193	One of a number of good plays. This one is merely a matter of taste.
8.	DEACNNG	SANG	L 10-13	+10 / 203	Purely for rack balance.
9.	DECNJIE	JI [B] E	1 L-O	+54 / 257	This one was easy.
10.	DECNLVO	LOVED	O 6-10	+32 / 289	B continues to make good plays.

GAME 3
DIAGRAM 3
FINAL POSITION

PLAYER A

	Rack	Word	Play Notation	Score
11.	QURMZAT	QUA	2 J-L	+41 279
12.	RMZTTNE	ZEE	9 M-O	+22 301
13.	RMTTNCO	CROP	D 3-6	+21 322
14.	MTTNDUI	DUC	B 1-3	+12

11. Easily the best play.

12. With only a few tiles remaining, A becomes afraid of being stuck with the Z, hence his play.

13. As good as any.

14. What else?
Remaining tiles: MTTNI
7 points × 2 = 14

Total 334

PLAYER B

	Rack	Word	Play Notation	Score
11.	CNRAENW	WAIF	I 1-4	+23 312
12.	CNRENES	OPENER	J 6-11	+8 320
13.	CNEESAK	CECA	3 B-E	+16 336
14.	NESK	KENS	12 G-J	+18 354 +14

11. Played solely for points.

12. Purely to keep a balanced rack.

13. Good play. B has counted A's tiles and sees he cannot profit from this play. Now B has two spots on the board to go out and win.

Total 368

Game 4

In this game, Player A's careless play makes what should have been a close match into a comfortable rout for his opponent.

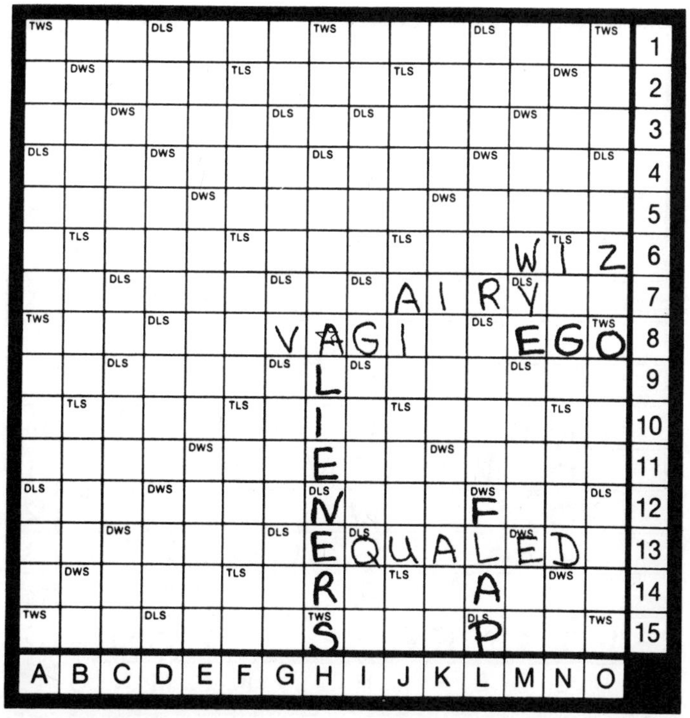
VAGI
AIRY
WIZ
EGO
ALIENERS
EQUALED
FLAP
A B C D E F G H I J K L M N O
1 2 3 4 5 6 7 8 9 10 11 12 13 14 15

GAME 4
DIAGRAM 1
Position after B's 4th turn.

PLAYER A

	Rack	Word	Play Notation	Score
1.	AAIIGVZ	VAGI	8 G-J	16

This is the best attempt to improve his rack without passing.

	Rack	Word	Play Notation	Score
2.	AIZEIRY	AIRY	7 J-M	+13 / 29

This play is justified by A's fine rack leave and his desire to play the Z for a high score.

	Rack	Word	Play Notation	Score
3.	ZEIAQUW	WIZ	6 M-O	+26 / 55

An interesting play. A is worried about two things: 1) the large spot he would have opened had he played GAZE N 8-11 and 2) the QW combination that would have been left in his rack. He, therefore, sacrifices 8 points for safety and flexibility. A good play.

	Rack	Word	Play Notation	Score
4.	EAQULID	EQUALED	13 H-N	+54 / 109

A had the Bingo QUAILED with no place to put it, so he settles for this 54 point play.

PLAYER B

Rack	Word	Play Notation	Score
DDDRRST	Pass DDDRRT		0

Poor tiles. Notice that B keeps the S.

Rack	Word	Play Notation	Score
SEEILOG	EGO	8 M-O	+17 / 17

These fine tiles just fall short of a Bingo so B keeps his rack balanced and places EGO on a triple word score.

Rack	Word	Play Notation	Score
SEILENR	ALIENERS	H 8-15	+77 / 94

A good draw results in this Bingo.

Rack	Word	Play Notation	Score
AEFPLRS	FLAP	L 12-15	+24 / 118

With his fine tiles, B keeps the board wide open in the hopes of another Bingo. Notice he does not neglect to score well.

GAME 4
DIAGRAM 2
Position after B's 8th turn.

PLAYER A					PLAYER B			
	Rack	Word	Play Notation	Score	Rack	Word	Play Notation	Score
5.	IAERVNU	PAVE	15 L-O	+27 / 136	ELRSELW	WAIL	J 6-9	+15 / 133

A cannot find anything better, so he uses the triple word score.

B decides against the Bingo possibility SWELLERS and rightly so. Instead he keeps his rack balanced and hopes for good tiles.

	Rack	Word	Play Notation	Score	Rack	Word	Play Notation	Score
6.	IRNUNMS	RUMEN	11 E-I	+14 / 150	ELRSETT	SETTLERS	15 A-H	+77 / 210

A poor rack induces this cautious play.

Another good draw brings another Bingo.

	Rack	Word	Play Notation	Score	Rack	Word	Play Notation	Score
7.	INSIONE	INION	10 B-F	+15 / 165	OOOKHET	NOOK	C 10-13	+16 / 226

Frustrated by his poor tiles, A makes this risky play to clear his rack.

This play is a diversion from B's real intention. He really wants to play HATE 14 K-N for 36 points but this would leave him with a very poor rack. So, in effect, he transposes his plays hoping that A will not block him on his next turn.

	Rack	Word	Play Notation	Score	Rack	Word	Play Notation	Score
8.	SEFAEAD	FA	D 12-13	+26 / 191	OHETBOO	HATE	14 K-N	+36 / 262

A obliges, but at a price. Notice that he does not play DAFT D 12-15 which would leave him with an imbalanced rack.

This play leaves B with a terrible rack but he is greedy for points. He has more or less decided to pass his next turn anyway.

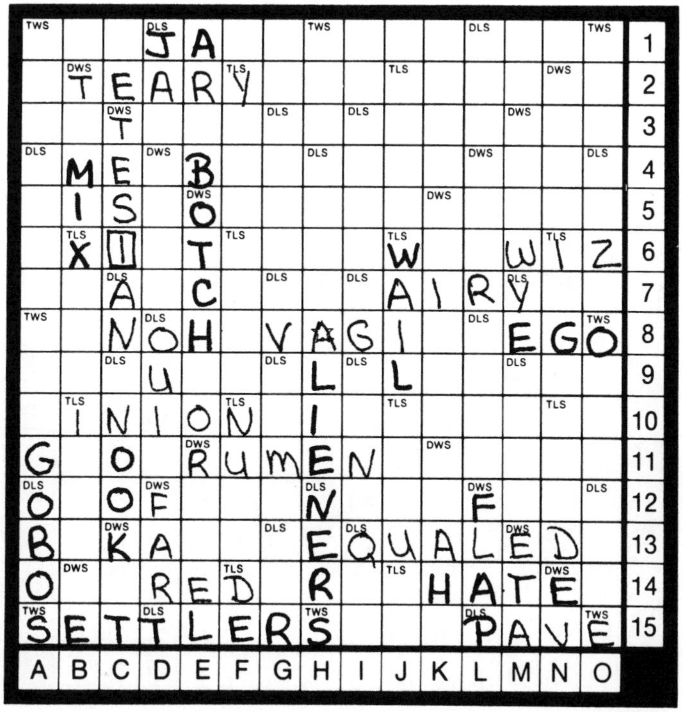

GAME 4
DIAGRAM 3
After B's 12th turn

PLAYER A

	Rack	Word	Play Notation	Score
9.	SEEADER	RED	14 D-F	+24 / 215

This play leaves an imbalanced rack but A needs these points to keep within range of his opponent.

	Rack	Word	Play Notation	Score
10.	SEEAOU□	OUI	D 8-10	+4 / 219

A is creating a spot for his potential Bingo.

	Rack	Word	Play Notation	Score
11.	SEEA□TN	ETES[I]AN	C 2-8	+70 / 289

A's tiles are very good, but this opens up a large play for the X on the square B-6. Better was EASTE[R]N in the same place.

	Rack	Word	Play Notation	Score
12.	AYURINT	TEARY	2 B-F	+32 / 321

Discouraged, A scores as best he can, but does not pay enough attention to the J spot he creates on D-1.

PLAYER B

Rack	Word	Play Notation	Score
OBOOBGI	GOBOS	A 11-15	+9 / 271

This play improves his rack and guards against (M)INION 10 A-F.

Rack	Word	Play Notation	Score
OBIATCH	BOTCH	E 4-8	+29 / 300

This play both blocks and scores.

Rack	Word	Play Notation	Score
IAXMISE	MIX	B 4-6	+58 / 358

A's careless play is immediately punished.

Rack	Word	Play Notation	Score
AISEJDC	JA	1 D-E	+36 / 394

B is relentlessly punishing his opponent for his carelessness.

GAME 4
DIAGRAM 4
FINAL POSITION

	PLAYER A				PLAYER B			
	Rack	Word	Play Notation	Score	Rack	Word	Play Notation	Score
13.	UINPD□	[S]PUD	10 J-M	+13 334	ISEDC	DISC	5 H-K	+22 416
	A plans to go out on the next play.							
14.	IN	BIN	4 E-G	+5 339 +2 Total 341		Remaining tile: E 1 point × 2 = 2		Total 416

Game 5

A difficult game with both players hindered by awkward racks. Each player comes up with clever answers to his problems but in the end, A prevails because of better tiles.

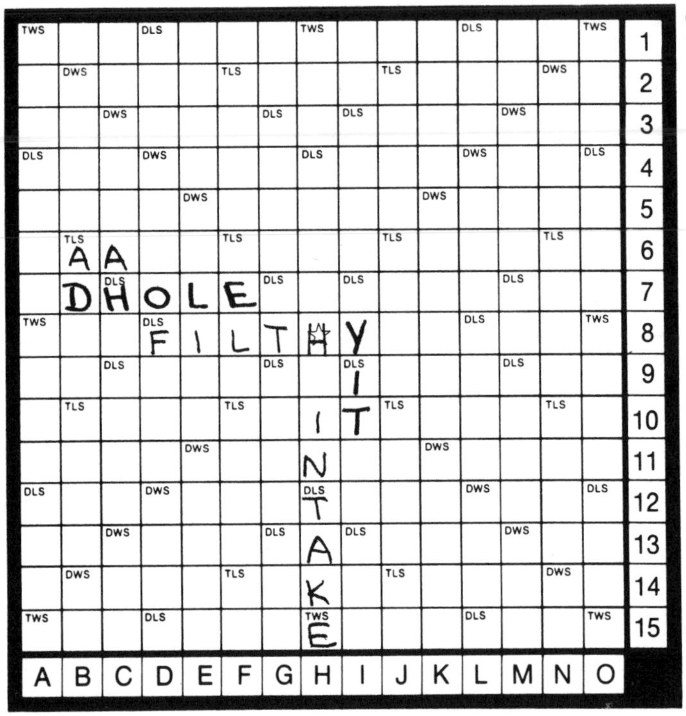

GAME 5
DIAGRAM 1
Position after B's 3rd turn

PLAYER A

	Rack	Word	Play Notation	Score
1.	TIKHLFI	FILTH	8 D-H	30

The most points and the best play.

	Rack	Word	Play Notation	Score
2.	IKAAAE□	AA	6 B-C	+14 44

Both good and bad. A uses this play to rid his rack of too many A's. He hopes his next draw will enable him to play a Bingo with his blank.

	Rack	Word	Play Notation	Score
3.	IKAE□TN	INTAKE	H 10-15	+35 79

B is in luck, as A doesn't challenge. Thinking his Bingo attempt thwarted (INTAKE[S] 9H-N), A takes advantage of the triple word score square H-15 opened up his opponent.

PLAYER B

Rack	Word	Play Notation	Score
HILEDGO	DHOLE	7 B-F	22

An alternate play was HILLOED F 6-12. B, however, did not want to leave a vowel next to the double word score square 11-E.

Rack	Word	Play Notation	Score
IGRIIYT	YIT	I 8-10	+22 44

In scoring 22 points with this phony word, B takes a chance that Player A won't challenge.

Rack	Word	Play Notation	Score
IGRIEEI	Pass 7		+ 0 44

Disagreeable as it seems, B must pass here as the duplication in his rack is likely to compound making his letters unplayable.

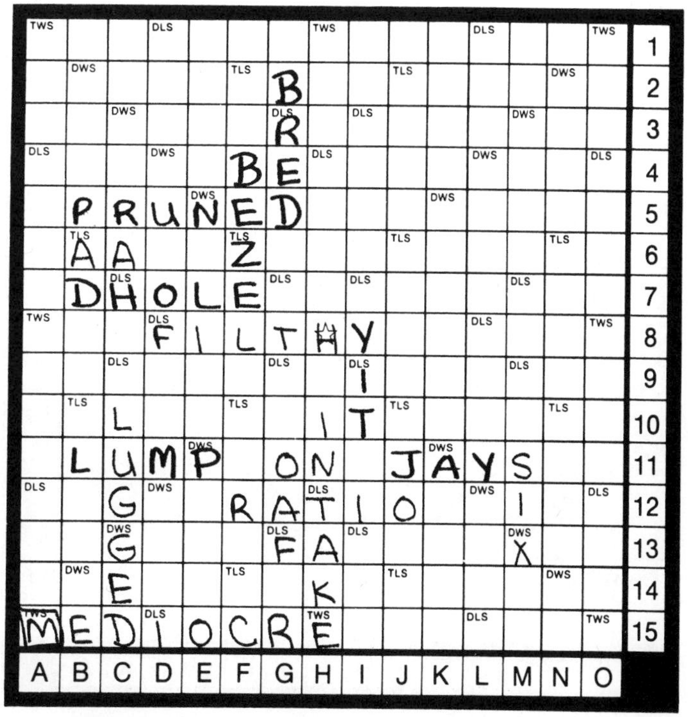

GAME 5
DIAGRAM 2
Position after B's 8th turn.

PLAYER A

	Rack	Word	Play Notation	Score
4.	□ARoroi	RATIO	12 F-J	+ 5 / 84
	A missed the Bingo [O] RATORIO 12 E-L, but balanced his rack with RATIO.			
5.	□ORCFOD	OAF	G 11-13	+21 / 105
	A prepares for his Bingo and picks up 21 points to boot.			
6.	□RCODEI	[M] EDIOCRE	15 A-H	+83 / 188
	Fine play.			
7.	GULGSIX	SIX	M 11-13	+34 / 222
	Perhaps not the best play from the viewpoint of rack leave, but A is in the lead. This play blocks the only S spot on the board for a Bingo. All in all, a wise play			
8.	GULGUEU	LUGGED	C 10-15	+18 / 240
	It is either this play or pass all seven.			

PLAYER B

Rack	Word	Play Notation	Score
ZPAEUJY	JAY	11 J-L	+35 / 79
A good draw in high-valued tiles. B uses the J for a neat 35 points.			
ZPEURNE	PRUNE	5 B-F	+26 / 105
This is a fine scoring play and leaves good tiles in the rack.			
ZEPBRRD	BEZEL	F 4-8	+36 / 141
B cleverly keeps his only vowel and still scores 36 points.			
EPRRDBE	BRED	G 2-5	+21 / 162
The alternatives BED G 3-5 and FADE 13 G-J, though more points are less preferable as B wants to balance his rack and catch up with a future Bingo.			
EPRLVNM	LUMP	11 B-E	+16 / 178
A bad draw prompts this somewhat risky play (clump, plump, slump) to keep a good rack leave.			

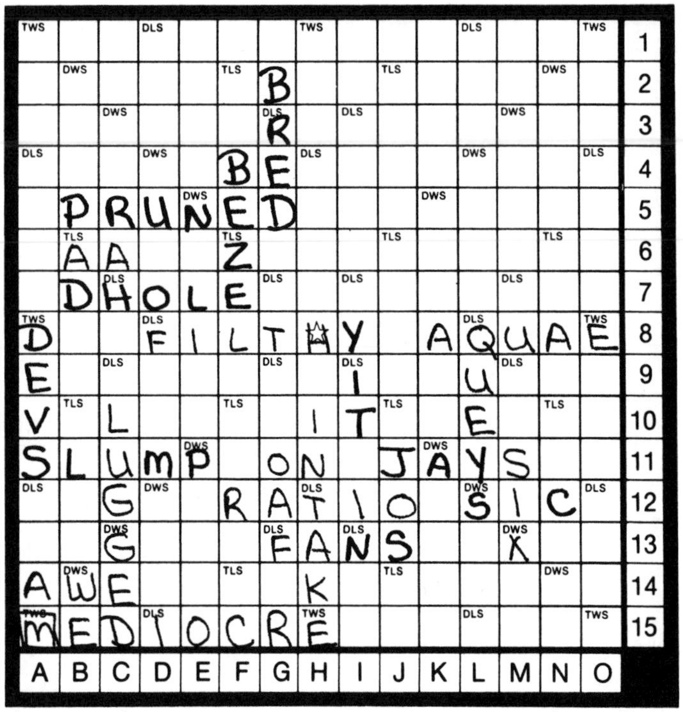

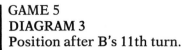

GAME 5
DIAGRAM 3
Position after B's 11th turn.

	PLAYER A Rack	Word	Play Notation	Score	PLAYER B Rack	Word	Play Notation	Score
9.	UUQTEER	QUEY	L 8-11	+26 / 266	ERVNSCS	SIC	12 L-N	+44 / 222
10.	UTERAAW	AQUAE	8 K-O	+42 / 308	ERVNSNS	FANS	13 G-J	+21 / 243
11.	TRWAOEI	AWE	14 A-C	+23 / 331	ERVNSDT	DEVS	A 8-11	+33 / 276

9. A: Good play. A risks the play on the double word square L-12 because he has the last U to use for the Q.

B: Naturally B does not refuse this excellent score.

10. A: Completing the idea of his previous play.

B: An unusual play. B plays away an S purely for the sake of balancing his rack. His decision appears to be valid in this case since a good draw would give him excellent Bingo possibilities.

11. A: There appears to be nothing better than this play.

B: Plagued by a lack of vowels, B finally relinquishes his last vowel in order to keep the score relatively close. He hopes he will draw at least one vowel.

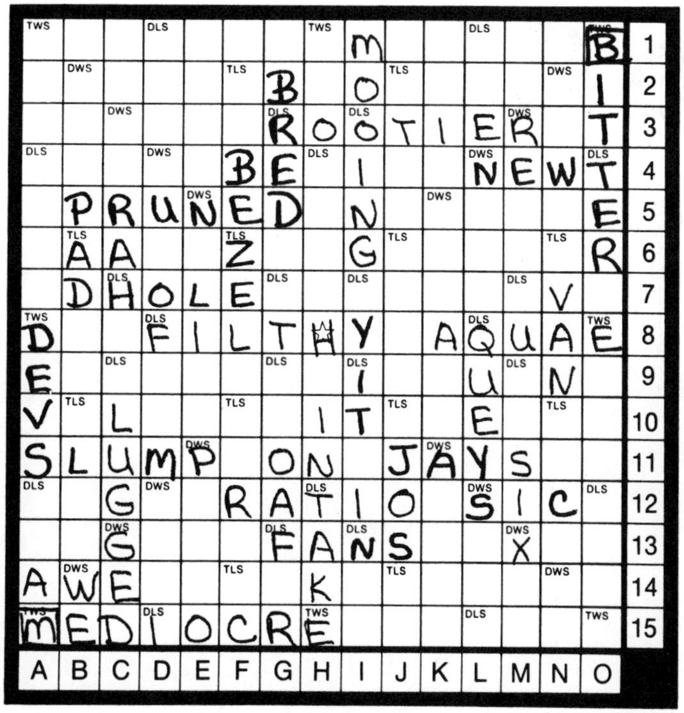

GAME 5
DIAGRAM 4
FINAL POSITION

PLAYER A

	Rack	Word	Play Notation	Score
12.	TROIIOE	ROOTIER	3 G-M	+16 / 347

Unlike B, A has too many vowels (a common situation) but with this neat play he clears his rack.

	Rack	Word	Play Notation	Score
13.	INNVOGM	VAN	N 7-9	+ 6 / 353

A plans to go out next turn.

	Rack	Word	Play Notation	Score
14.	INOGM	MOOING	I 1-16	+ 9 / 362 / + 4

Total 366

PLAYER B

Rack	Word	Play Notation	Score
RNTWITE	NEWT	4 L-O	+22 / 298

Discouraged by not being able to play his Bingo, B makes this uninspired move. Since all the large tiles have been played he probably won't be hurt by this play.

Rack	Word	Play Notation	Score
RITAOE□	B ITTER	O 1-6	+15 / 313

Now with several Bingos, B still has no spots to play them. He does the best he can.

Remaining tiles: A, O
2 points x 2 = 4

Total 313

Game 6

A fairly well played game where A's better tiles prevail.

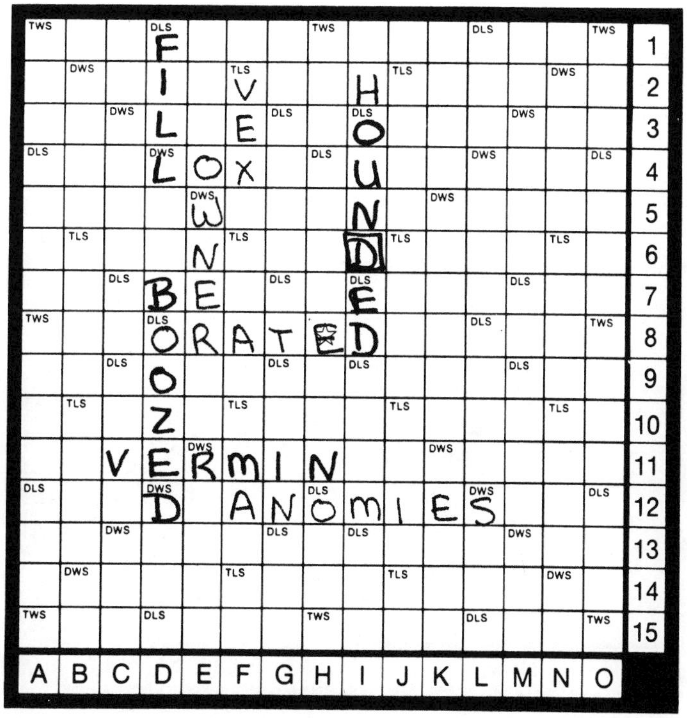

GAME 6
DIAGRAM 1
Position after B's 4th turn.

PLAYER A

	Rack	Word	Play Notation	Score
1.	TEEAROO	ORATE	8 D-H	12
	Player A considered passing all seven tiles or only OOE ("fishing"). Any of these three plays is acceptable.			
2.	EOEWXEN	OWNER	E 4-8	+20 / 32
	A could have played OXEN 9 G-J but didn't want to give B the opportunity to play near the X. Nevertheless, that play is at least as acceptable as the one made, since B could just as easily use the double word square D-4 to his advantage.			
3.	EEXVONS	VEX	F 2-4	+31 / 63
	FOXES 1 D-H would have been better.			
4.	EONSMIA	ANOMIES	12 F-L	+79 / 142
	Good play.			

PLAYER B

Rack	Word	Play Notation	Score
DOZENBM	BOOZED	D 7-12	36
This play gives the most points and tile turnover.			
NMVILLF	FILL	D 1-4	+26 / 62
B scores some points and, perhaps dangerously opens up the board.			
NMVIDR□	VERMIN	11 C-H	+22 / 84
Too many consonants for a Bingo.			
D□UNHOE	HOUN[D]ED	I 2-8	+69 / 153
Good play.			

GAME 6
DIAGRAM 2
After B's 8th turn.

PLAYER A

	Rack	Word	Play Notation	Score
5.	RAIIGS□	RAISI[N]GS	L 5-12	+59 / 201
	A has drawn Bingo tiles and plays his second in a row.			
6.	GAUYYLS	GAILY	J 10-14	+21 / 222
	An attempt to balance an awkward rack. Perhaps the play YAY F 7-9 getting rid of both Y's would have been better.			
7.	UYSARAE	AY	10 F-G	+20 / 242
	A has limited choices with these poor tiles. AY improves his rack although not ideally.			
8.	USRAECE	CAUSERIE	N 2-9	+74 / 316
	This fine Bingo puts A way in the lead.			

PLAYER B

Rack	Word	Play Notation	Score
WROUPIG	POW	H 1-3	+34 / 187
Despite awkward tiles, B finds a high scoring play.			
RUIGFLI	GUFF	1 A-D	+33 / 220
RIFF 1 A-D was better as it avoids duplication of I's in the rack.			
RILIDET	SLID	8 L-O	+15 / 235
B opens up the board somewhat, but keeps good tiles in his rack.			
RIETBID	NOTED	H 11-15	+18 / 253
A little disheartened B could not find anything better.			

GAME 6
DIAGRAM 3
FINAL POSITION

PLAYER A

	Rack	Word	Play Notation	Score
9.	OUTPORT	TROOP	K 2-6	+22 / 338
10.	UTSTENN	GET	11 L-N	+4 / 342
11.	UTSNNAA	VAN	C 11-13	+15 / 357
12.	UTSNACE	SCENT	O 11-15	+35 / 392
13.	UAQ	QUID	15 E-H	+14

9. A holds onto his U as the Q is still unplayed.

10. A doesn't see any high scoring play, so he tries to set himself up for the TWS at 15-O (since other S's and blanks are out). His rack leave is so poor that he may not be able to take advantage of the spot he opened up.

11. A creates a spot for QUAD 12 A-D and balances his rack.

12. A's plans are working perfectly.

13. Remaining tile: A
1 point × 2 = 2

Total 406

PLAYER B

	Rack	Word	Play Notation	Score
9.	RIBIJIT	JAB	3 M-O	+24 / 277
10.	RIIITAE	ID	15 G-H	+3 / 280
11.	RIITAEH	TI	2 K-L	+2 / 282
12.	RITAEHK	HIKE	B 12-15	+31 / 313
13.	RTA	TARN	14 L-O	+8 / 321 / +2

9. This play leaves very poor tiles in B's rack but he doesn't want to pass up the points and has no good alternates.

10. With only seven tiles left and the Q still out, B cautiously plays only one tile, the duplicating I.

11. B creates a spot for his H and sticks to his previous policy of playing one letter at a time.

12. B's plans are working, too, but he's not scoring enough points.

Total 323

Part 7

Reader's Quiz

All players are invited to test their expertise with the Reader's Quiz. These problems illustrate various principles discussed in the Handbook. Please consider the answers carefully as some plays have alternative solutions.

Quiz
DIAGRAM 1

1. Find the highest point count play.

RACK
AIHTFVG

FAITH 12 H-L for 55 points. Player A uses both the double letter and double word squares (see Chapter 7-B).

Quiz
DIAGRAM 2

2. Find the best play with an X.

RACK
AOILXTN

LOX 2 H-J for 61 points. Player A uses the triple letter square (2-J) for maximum point count (see Chapter 7-B).

FAIREST
HA
BEGONE
A B C D E F G H I J K L M N O

Quiz
DIAGRAM 3

3. Here is the board before Player B's second turn. Given the rack, AGGINPT, Player B is considering the play, PAGE L3-6 for 14 points. Are there any better plays?

RACK
AGGINPT

Both GRATING K 5-11 for 36 points and PRATING K 5-11 for 40 points are better (see Chapter 11).

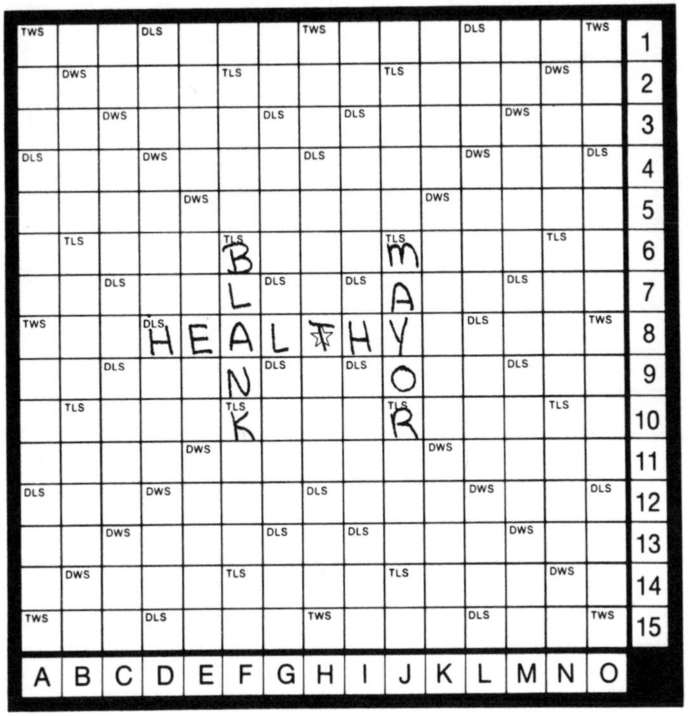

BLANK
MAYOR
HEALTHY
A B C D E F G H I J K L M N O

Quiz
DIAGRAM 4

4. Your opponent has just played BLANK F 6-10 and is developing a Bingo rack. How would you block the board?

RACK
TILEDQS

TITLED H 6-11 for 7 points blocks the major letters on the board (see Chapter 13-A).

Quiz
DIAGRAM 5

5. What's the best play?

RACK
GENFIRS

LIMPID
FICHU
RIGID

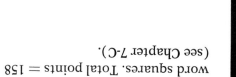

REFUSING O 1-8 using two triple word squares. Total points = 158 (see Chapter 7-C).

Quiz
DIAGRAM 6

6. Your opponent has just played OPERATE B 8-14. How would you block the O adjacent to the triple word square (8-A)?

RACK
FOECMER

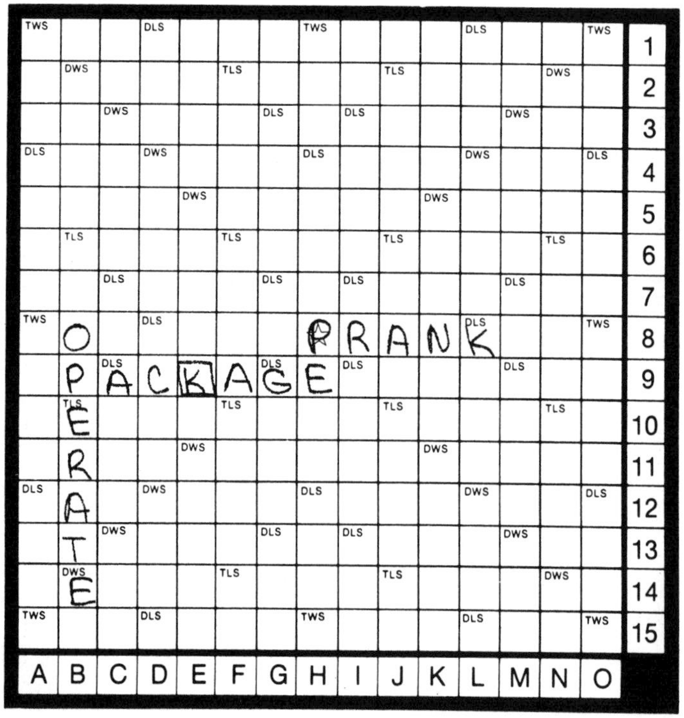

OPERATE
PACKAGE
PRANK

FAME C 8-11 for 20 points. This clearly occupies the most dangerous spot (see Chapter 12-B-2).

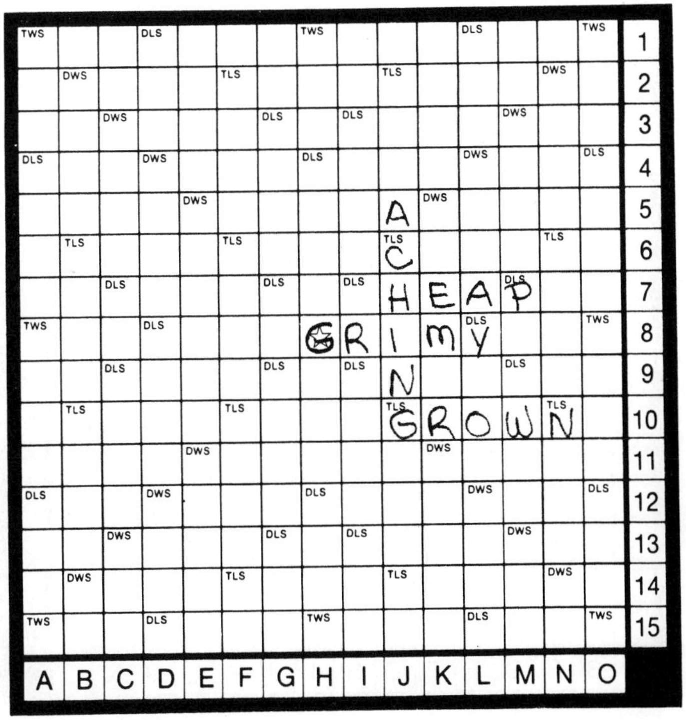

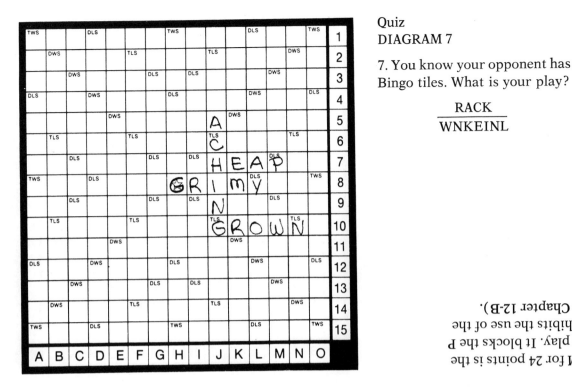

Quiz
DIAGRAM 7

7. You know your opponent has Bingo tiles. What is your play?

RACK
WNKEINL

WĀKEN 5 I-M for 24 points is the best blocking play. It blocks the P on M-7 and inhibits the use of the G on H-8 (see Chapter 12-B).

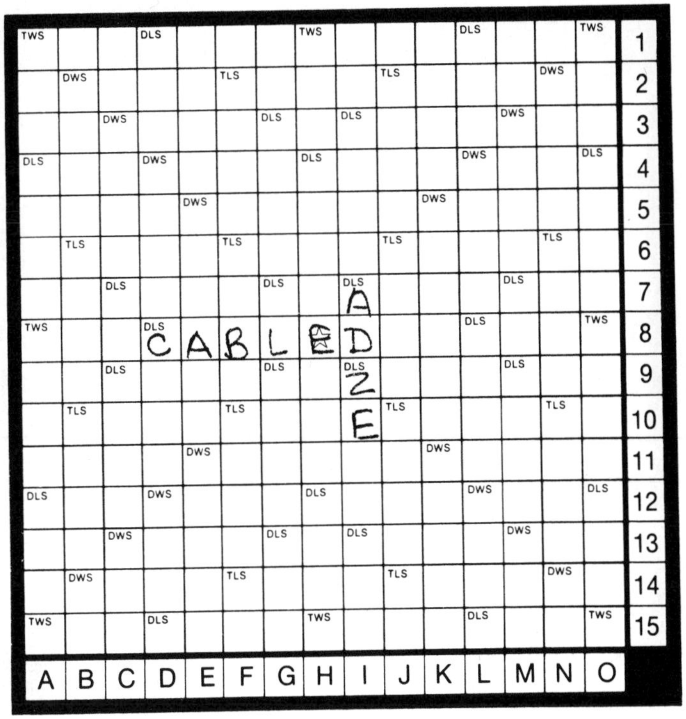

Quiz
DIAGRAM 8

8. What is the best play?

RACK
PASSEL□

PLEAS[E]S 11 E-K for 97 points is the best play as it tends to block the board. PASSĀ[B]LE E 4-11 for 86 points opens up the board (see Chapter 13-A).

Quiz
DIAGRAM 9

9. What would you play?

RACK
AAAFRRC

MOATS
ADDUCE

FARAD D 4-8 for 18 points to get rid of the duplication. This also creates a spot for the last A on square C-7 (see Chapter 8-B).

Quiz
DIAGRAM 10

10. Your opponent has just played LIGATION H 6-15 for 60 points. Do you challenge?

BLUNGED
LIGATION

No. Look for other Bingos in these letters. Your opponent could have played DILATION, LIBATION, or ILLATION. By the way, LIGATION is good (see Chapter 16).

Quiz
DIAGRAM 11

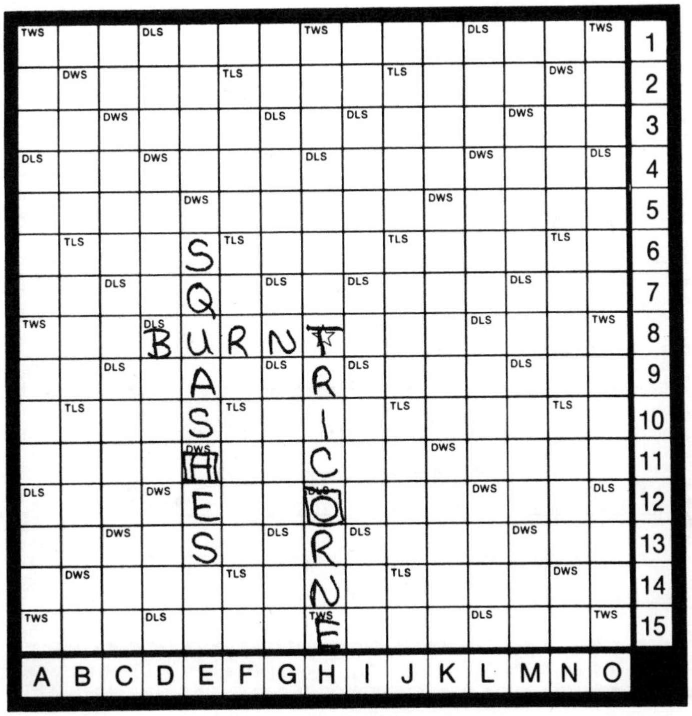
SQUASHES
BURNT
TRICORNE

11. What is your play?

RACK
NVNETSU

There are two possibilities: a) SUNBURNT 8 A-H for 30 points, or b) UNBURNT 8 B-H for 9 points. The latter has more potential and is more troublesome to your opponent, as you hold the last S and can open the triple word square at A-1 or A-15 (see Chapter 7-C).

Quiz
DIAGRAM 12

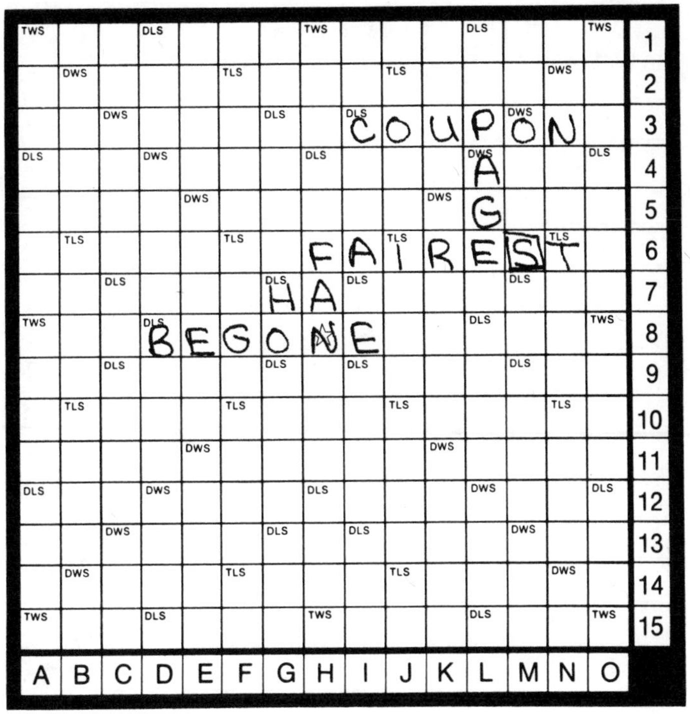
COUPON
PAGE
FAIREST
HA
BEGONE

12. Look for the possible Bingos.

RACK
EGILRNT

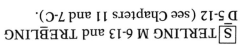

[S]TERLING M 6-13 and TREBLING D 5-12 (see Chapters 11 and 7-C).

Quiz
DIAGRAM 13

13. What is your play?

RACK
WAAITAJ

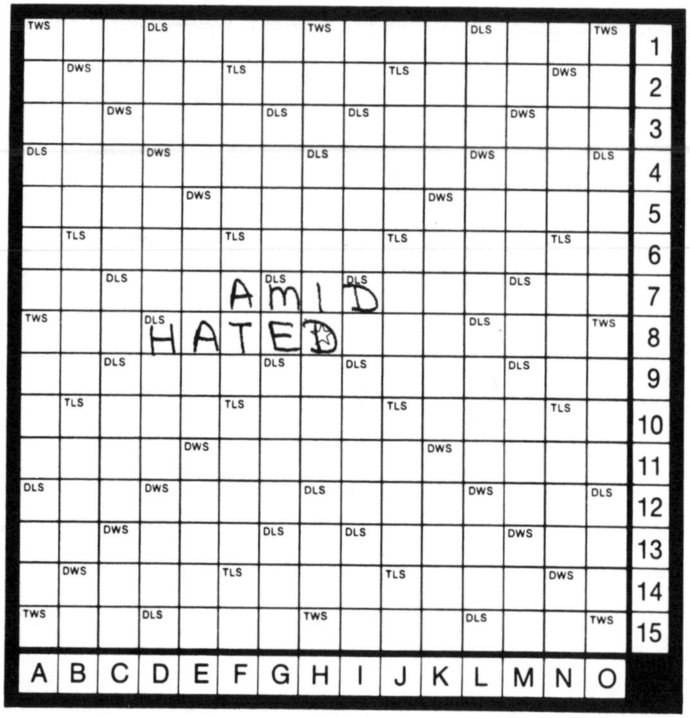
AMID
HATED

AWAIT 6 I-M for 19 points is recommended, as the plays JAW or TAW 6 D-F leave very poor tiles in the rack. This particular play creates a spot for the J on the double word square K-5 (see Chapter 8-A).

Quiz
DIAGRAM 14

14. What is a good dynamic play?

RACK
AIEFDLA

BROAD
WAXY

AIDE 9 D-G for 12 points opens up the one for one principle. When your opponent gets a high scoring play, you can counterscore with one of your own (see Chapter 12-A-6).

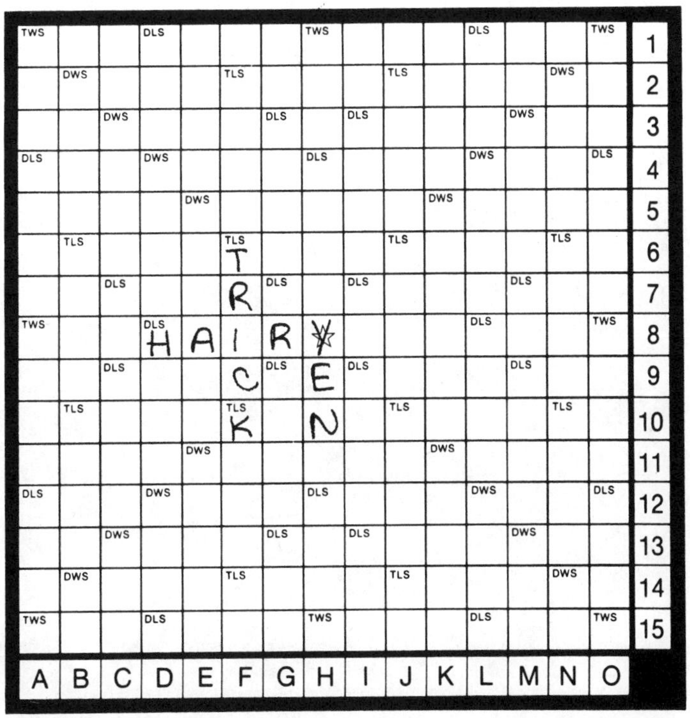

Quiz
DIAGRAM 15

15. Your opponent has just played YEN H 8-10. What play do you make?

RACK
LSGWNOY

Your opponent obviously has Bingo-conducive tiles and is fishing for a tile he needs. Therefore, the recommended play is SNOWY 11 H-L for 29 points. The S on square 11-H acts defensively while the line of play along 11 forces an opponent to make Bingos of 8 or more letters (see Chapter 13-A).

Quiz
DIAGRAM 16

16. Player B wants to play AT 4 L-M for 5 points. If you were player B, what play would you make?

RACK
ESITTU□

[S] ITU [A] TES M 6-13 (see Chapters 7-C and 9-D).

Helpful Lists

Part 8

4. Words Using Higher-Valued Tiles

Below is a short list of words using higher-valued tiles. Additional lists are published in the SCRABBLE PLAYERS Newspaper (See page 12).

F	H	J	K	Q	W	X	Y	Z
clef	horizon	ajee	jake	jonquil	jigsaw	axes	oxygen	adze
eyeful	hubcap	conjure	jink	quack	oxbow	axis	phony	azan
faze	humbler	djinni	kabob	quake	squawks	duplex	phooey	bizarre
flaxen	hunk	janty	kaolin	quartz	swami	extreme	yacht	blaze
foxhole	hurry	jefe	kapok	quetzal	tweeze	ilex	yahoo	breeze
franc	hwan	jereed	kedge	queue	waltz	pharynx	yammers	kazoo
frozen	jihad	jeux	kelp	quiet	waxy	unisex	yarrow	phiz
hefty	phlox	jewelry	kerf	quite	yawn	xebec	yawl	sneeze
wharf	phobia	jiffy	ketch	quiz	yawper	xylyl	yclept	zarf
yaff	squash	jumble	kylix	squeeze	ywis	xyst	yucca	zebu

5. Two-Letter Words

Below is a list of the acceptable two-letter words. This list will increase when the SCRABBLE PLAYERS Dictionary is completed (See page 81).

aa	by	id	mu	pi
ad	de	if	my	re
ae	do	in	na	si
ah	eh	is	no	so
ai	el	it	nu	ti
am	em	ja	od	to
an	en	jo	of	up
ar	ex	ka	oh	us
as	fa	la	on	ut
at	go	li	or	we
ax	ha	lo	os	wo
ay	he	ma	ox	xi
ba	hi	me	pa	ye
be	ho	mi	pe	

6. Three Letter Words

Below are some good three-letter words to know.

aal	cay	fax	hoy	lei	nee	pye	tau	von
aba	cee	fen		lek	nib	pyx	tav	vug
aby	col	fet	ism	leu	nob		taw	
adz	cos	feu		lev	nog	qua	ted	wab
aga	cox	fey	jag	lex	noh		teg	wae
ain	coz	fid	jeu	ley	nom	rad	tew	wap
ait		fiz	jew	loo	noo	raj	tho	wat
ala	dag	fob	joe	lum	nth	rax	til	wen
alp	dak	foh	jow	lux		rei	tod	wha
ama	dap	fon	jus		obe	rem	tom	wis
ami	daw	foy		mae	obi	rep	too	wiz
amu	dev		kab	mag	oho	ret	tor	wop
ana	dey	gad	kae	maw	oka	rev	tun	wot
ane	dol	gae	kay	mel	oot	rex	tup	wye
ani	dor	gar	kea	mho	ope	rin	twa	
auk	duc	ged	kef	mib	orc	roc		yep
ava	dup	gey	ken	mig	ort		udo	yew
ave		gib	kep	mil	ose	sab	ugh	yin
awa	eau	gid	kex	mir	oui	sal	uit	yod
awn	ecu	gie	kip	moa		sec		yon
azo	edh	gip	kop	mol	pam	sen	vas	yow
	eft	goa	kor	mon	pas	sib	vau	yuk
bel	eld		kos	mot	phi	sic	vav	
ben	eme	hae		mun	piu	syn	vaw	zoa
bey	emu	haj	lac	mut	pix		vet	
bis	ern	het	lar		poi	tae	vin	
bot	eta	hie	lea	nae	psi	taj	vis	
bur	eth	hod	lee	neb	pur	tam	voe	

All the words in the preceding lists are found in Funk & Wagnalls Standard College Dictionary, 1973-74 edition. See page 81 for details of the SCRABBLE PLAYERS Dictionary.

Part 9

Glossary

BALANCING
An attempt to keep an equal number of vowels and consonants in the rack without duplication.

BINGO
A play using all seven tiles for a 50-point bonus. Also called a Bonus word.

BLOCKING
Closing a section of the board to an opponent's Bingo attempt or high scoring play.

BLUFF
Deliberately playing a phony word.

CHALLENGE
Disputing the validity of an opponent's play. In club and tournament play, one of the players loses his turn when there's a challenge (see Chapter 4).

COUNTING
Keeping track mentally of which tiles have been played and which have not.

DUPLICATION
Having two or more of the same letter in a player's rack.

FISHING
Playing away or passing one or two tiles for the sole purpose of getting a Bingo.

GAMBIT
A sacrifice of points for rack development or position on the board.

HOOK
A letter or word on the board to which a player can attach another word.

LEAVE
The tiles that are left in the rack after making a play.

PASSING
Taking a turn to exchange some, all, or no tiles.

PHONY
A fabricated word which, if challenged, will cause the player to lose his turn.

PREMIUM SQUARES
The colored squares on the board that can double or triple the value of a letter or word.

RACK
The seven tiles a player has before making a play.